Catfish on Fridays

A View from Inside the U.S Government Financial Management Swamp

Steve MacQueen

Second Edition: June 2019

Kindle Direct Publishing.

Table of Contents

Preface

This book is non-fiction but there are many stories. The stories are true but the names used are fictional, mainly because I don't want to embarrass anyone, especially myself by getting sued. I've made a lot of friends over the course of my career and also respect the work they've done, for the most part. This book deals mostly with "the other part." Even though the thrust of this book deals with finance, government accounting and the like, I dumbed the technical parts down a bit and tried to make it interesting so everyone can understand what I'm talking about. I know you'll run into some pretty technical areas that may cause you to give up, but don't! That's where the gold is buried. If you take it slow and digest that material, you'll appreciate how revolutionary yet uncomplicated my solutions to fixing government finance really are. Alternatively, just skip over those chapters since I summarize my conclusions at the end of the book.

In theory, more books will be sold if I exposed the secret sex scandals rocking the federal government to its core, but I didn't run across any of that. What I did see is theft; a lot of theft...... from you, the American taxpayer. Even if you didn't pay federal income taxes last year you should still be very concerned about the billions of dollars being wasted by the federal government every year. If that waste was reduced, even by half, there would be more money available to spend on the the things you would actually benefit from.

There is one thing that is very important to understand as you read this book. I'm not trying to belittle anyone or disparage them in any way. We're all pretty much equal when it comes to our living our lives and our contribution to society. Sure there are exceptions. Much like the normal distribution curve in statistics, most everyone is in the middle somewhere; and in the one tail of the curve, say one percent, are the really intelligent and creative people like Albert Einstein and Leonardo DaVinci. At the other end are the sociopathic murderers, rapists, etc. I believe that basically nobody is really smart or really dumb. It's what I call the law of offsetting talents.

The vast majority of us have things we are really good at and things we are not so good at. For example, my strengths are in things like financial reporting and writing for clarity[1]. On the other hand, I am very awkward in a social setting; I'm basically invisible at a party, and rarely get invited. I can't carry a tune; I am horrible with expressing my emotions except when I lose my temper. Some people have the drive and ambition to become rich, famous and/or aspire to hold high political office. Others are content to be happy and make others happy regardless of social standing and wealth. Some are care givers and some could care less.

Most of the people I single out in this book with anecdotal stories are what I refer to as trying to fit a square peg in a round hole. They are part of the vast empire of federal

---

[1] Note that for clarity and ease of reading I end a lot of sentences with prepositions, even though it was Winston Churchill who said that "Ending a sentence with a preposition is something up with which I will not put!"

employees; mostly all good people but unfortunately are working in a job beneath their true capabilities in other areas. And they are doing it with your hard earned taxpayer money, a lot of it.

I have no axe to grind by publishing this book. I retired under my own terms and even got a bonus for sticking around longer than I originally planned. My purpose is to give people outside the government a glimpse of what happens inside the government and perhaps provide the impetus for making some common sense changes to how the government operates, and in particular Federal Financial Management.

At the time of this writing I am 66 years old and still haven't figured out what I want to do when I grow up. I guess you could say I'm an accounting and finance professional, having worked for about 40 years in that line of work. However, I choose not to define myself by how I've made a living but how I've lived my life and this book is about sharing some of those experiences with you.

So, here I am, finally getting around to writing this book I've been thinking about ever since I spent my first day working for the United States government as a civilian, about 13 years ago. Some of what I am about to tell you may be written in books all over the place but I don't have a clue because personally, I would never want to read about the life of a federal employee...how boring. This book is not just about the life of a federal employee; in fact, it's more about what happens inside that huge bureaucracy day in and day out...your precious tax dollars at work. So, hang in there and I'll get to the catfish part of the story in Chapter 17.

Chapter 1 – A Cushy Government Job

Most of us working stiffs have wondered what it would be like having a government job at one point or another, except for those who actually do work for the government. The first time I seriously thought about it was when I was working within commuting distance to Washington D.C., in the fast-paced, sophisticated area called southern Maryland, Calvert County in particular. When the company I was working for was getting bought-out, my staff started talking about how good it would be to get a government job. It was really hard to do because so many people wanted one. I was thinking about why that might be when I remembered my short stint in the Army…that was government. And they were paying me to go to school. If actually working for the government was anything like what I experienced at Fort Benjamin Harrison, Indiana (they called it the country club of the Army), it's no wonder people wanted to work there.

Now let me give you a little background about my work ethic growing up. I hated to work; but I loved making money, mostly because I never had much. I remember shoveling snow as a kid all day and making a couple dollars. Folding money was a big deal back then. Even getting an "eagle quarter" to shovel the end of a driveway (you know, where the snow plows pile up the snow real deep) was deeply rewarding. I grew up in a family of five children and getting an allowance was something only the kids on the other side of town were getting. So when I couldn't "borrow" money from my mom's purse or secret hiding places, I had to find work if I wanted something cool, like a BB gun or a Duncan yo-yo. As a young kid I would try anything to make a buck from delivering newspapers to selling seeds and greeting cards door to door. As I got old enough to earn an hourly wage some of my jobs included work at: Tastee-Freeze; Jack-in-the-Box (where I got my first raise in pay from $1.50 to $1.75 per hour after working there for only about a month); Shraft's Restaurant, as a breakfast cook; Delaware Park Racetrack, parking cars; an apartment complex maintenance man; construction foreman's helper; liquor store clerk; and my favorite, assistant chef at a girls summer camp in Harrison, Maine when I was 17 years old.

I know, you're probably thinking everyone has hard luck stories. I have to admit that I didn't have it all bad. I wasn't starving, and was pushed off to school every day and managed to hang out with the good kids mostly all the way through school. And between my parents and Aunt, my college was mostly paid for. Or so I thought, until after I graduated and found a decent job, my father handed me the loan that was not yet paid off. What a great dad! But all kidding aside, I do thank my parents for teaching me the value of a buck...the hard way.

My career in the accounting and finance world was helped along by my impressive college grade-point average of 2.7, and rounded up that's a B average, right? I spent more time at keg parties than going to class and waking up just in time for lunch was a regular routine. I started out as an engineering major, but very soon realized that taking calculus, chemistry and computer science for engineers all in one semester[2] was certain failure, especially when the teachers assumed you already knew the material; and most of the other students actually did know it, because they were in the "advanced" classes in high school. Wasn't that something a guidance counselor should have told me? I knew we had guidance counselors but I don't know of any classmate who actually talked to one.

In any event, I did actually buckle-down for my last semester and made the Dean's list, seriously. I always had a knack for math and made a great move switching to an accounting major early on in my academic career. So now, off to find a job as an Accountant. My Reserve Officers Training Corps (ROTC) commitment to the Army, however, put that on hold for a few months while I attended the Finance Officers Basic Course at Fort Benjamin Harrison in Indiana.

That was a totally different Army than the Army I experienced at Ft. Bragg, North Carolina for basic training. I was going to school for 90 days learning how Army finance works (essentially military pay). It was so boring that's where I learned to drink coffee all day like everyone else and the only thing military about the experience was that each one of us got a turn being Officer of the Day for the installation. Now that was pretty cool. We sat by the telephone at night in case any emergencies arose. I actually did get a call and contacted the Military Police to break up a

---

[2] I do want to take the opportunity to thank those professors and grad students who thoroughly turned me off to college early on. Part of the credit also goes to the fine institution of the University of Delaware, without whom I would not have mastered the arts of beer drinking, making wombats, and "pennying" your roommate inside the dorm room.

fight at the Officers Club. I guess you could say that was the only real action I saw during my three months active duty for training and eight years in the Army Reserves.

After Fort "Ben" I figured I ought to start looking for a real job using my accounting degree. I didn't want to live at my parent's house one day more than I had to. Job hunting in those days was totally different without the internet. But networking was always the most valuable tool so I was lucky enough to get a tip from a friend that Columbia Gas was hiring. I got dressed up, put my resume in a cheap brief case and simply walked into their headquarters building in ritzy Greenville Delaware; no appointment. The state of Delaware truly is a small wonder. Wouldn't you know it…the Supervisor with whom I interviewed just happened to be married to a girl I knew of in high school. I guess I said the right things and a couple days later I got a phone call offering me a job for $10,000 per year. Ka Ching!

The company paid for my Masters Degree in Finance, taking classes at night, and up the ladder I went, slowly but surely.

Chapter 2 - A Quick Synopsis of my Private Sector Career, before Joining the Government

Private sector experience provides a good basis for comparison to government work. I spent 30 years working for a Fortune 500 diversified energy corporation. That was way too long...but it added stability to my life and allowed me to raise a great family, buy a nice house in the country and lead a comfortable lifestyle. But all good things must come to an end, and before I got to retirement age the company got bought out by another, albeit smaller, utility. At the time I was the financial controller for a joint venture project between the company I worked for (Columbia Energy at the time) and the Potomac Electric Power Company (PEPCO). Now this is a good little story.

The joint venture was formed by units of Columbia and PEPCO to make use of a liquefied natural gas (LNG) import facility that had been idle for many years, since the Algerian suppliers would rather cut the supplies than renegotiate a lower export price. PEPCO chipped in cash and Columbia provided the mothballed facilities sited on the edge of the Chesapeake Bay. The idea was to build a liquefaction unit that operated during the summer, to fill the huge existing LNG storage tanks on site. Then, during the winter, the process was reversed by heating the LNG and sending it out on the coldest days of winter (called peak-shaving).

Ultimately, if the demand for natural gas in the United States improved enough, the import terminal would be recommissioned. This consisted of a huge deep water pier facility in the Chesapeake Bay connected to shore via an underwater tunnel tube about one mile long. The relationship between the two partners at the beginning was very cooperative since the peak-shaving business was selling out year after year. We got together for strategy sessions and dinners to celebrate our success.

However, when the domestic gas futures market started to look promising and extra money was needed to make the right business contacts to potentially develop the LNG import business, PEPCO's position was ultra-conservative. Their managing Partner referred to Columbia's business development travel as "your nickel". Needless to say, their management didn't think much of the future of LNG imports; so as the peaking business started to tail off, it wasn't long before the two partners had a falling-out. This was very entertaining from my vantage point, since the two top executives would do most of the arguing and the PEPCO exec was quite the screamer. Once you got to know him well enough, you figured out he was actually a nice guy, but man could he yell. The irony of the situation was that PEPCO's reluctance to take risks was actually playing right into the hands of Columbia.

To make a long story short, after much wrangling and gnashing of teeth Columbia ended up offering PEPCO $50 million (a nice premium) for their half of the business. Several months later Columbia, now having both halves, "Park Place *and* Boardwalk", sold the entire facility for $200 million. I would have loved to hear the screaming at PEPCO when they found they left $50 million on the table. But so nobody gets sued, it was totally on the up and up; no prior deal to sell the entire facility was even considered until after the PEPCO buyout.

Once the facility was sold, I was fortunate enough to have an opportunity with another Columbia project being operated out of Northern Virginia. So, I didn't even have to consider moving, as what was left of the headquarters operation of Columbia was relocated to the hotspot of Merrillville, Indiana. This new project was a situation where Columbia was attempting to make use of the rights-of-way it already had for its pipelines, and parlay that into non-regulated business income from the laying of fiber optic cable and perhaps even getting into the business of operating a lit (operational) fiber optic network. They had grandiose plans. I remember running business scenarios where our fiber was covering the entire Middle Eastern seaboard. Unfortunately, the timing was bad…real bad.

The telecom market had just begun to implode (in 2001) and on top of that the company was ordered to cease laying fiber by the Army Corps of Engineers. Some fiber laying crew had inadvertently stepped on an endangered bog turtle habitat while crossing some marshlands. They may as well have sunk in quicksand.

When my boss and I came on board, our objective was to pull the project that was essentially derailed, out of the ditch, complete the cable line from Washington DC to New York, and then sell it and get the hell out of dodge before any more money was lost. Unfortunately, the place was being run amuck with telecom "professionals" that had been used to spending money wildly because that's what had to be done to be a "player in that space" (so we were told). As Vice President of Finance, I had to keep close watch on what was being spent and boy was that a tough job. We were paying consultants a minimum of $150 per hour, some just to do clerical work. And the telecom engineers would be out wining and dining each other on travel, making it seem like necessary business expenditures. I recall one incident where we actually checked up on an expense statement receipt described as a "PATH site tour", a tunnel in New Jersey and New York where the fiber had to be laid. The "tour" actually consisted of a strip club bill in the hundreds of dollars for this guy and his cronies. This same guy would take his wife on travel and bill her "aroma therapy spa" sessions to the company…what guts!

There is one more thing about this telecom gig that was an unexpected benefit. When we were winding up the eventual completion of the project, my boss (the President) got a call from a lawyer in Georgia. He needed someone to assist with some testimony in connection with a lawsuit involving another natural gas facility. It was finance related, so he referred the lawyer to me. Since I was leaving soon anyway, it was not a conflict of interest. When the lawyer asked me what my billing rate was, being so impressed by what these telecom folks were getting, I threw out a figure of $175 per hour (much much higher than I was actually making). He responded, "well, that's what I'm making, so it shouldn't be a problem". Ask and ye shall receive!

Chapter 3 - Independent Contracting

I'm getting to the part about the government job but there is one more tour of duty I went through, that actually had prepared me better for the government. This was an independent consulting gig with Washington Gas. After the telecom assignment wrapped up I needed a break and actually could afford to take a break since I got a pretty good severance package. Then, not having the financial means to retire quite yet, I applied for a Controller position I saw advertised by one of our previous competitors, Washington Gas. A couple of weeks later, I got a phone call from a friend and former business associate of mine. It turns out that he already got the job I had applied for but he wanted me to come in to discuss a consulting gig. Again, networking at its finest, but without me making a single phone call.

Washington Gas actually did prepare me for a government job in many respects. Their central office was a big run-down building in the middle of Washington DC. The office staff was very diverse and there were so many of them it was hard to get to know all of them and what they did. Everyone I met there was very friendly and helpful except for one guy who eventually threw me out of his office.

It was my job to dig into the accounting for a certain activity that I can't really discuss in detail but partly involved loaning money to employees for gas appliance purchases etc. It was one of those activities that required some complex accounting for some pretty basic transactions. Since Washington Gas was a publicly traded company, it had to follow Generally Accepted Accounting Principles promulgated by the Financial Accounting Standards Board (the FASB) and the financial reporting rules of the Securities and Exchange Commission (the SEC). The external auditors of the company deemed this loan activity significant enough to fall under the rules that applied to large financial institutions loaning money…so ridiculous.

In any event, I had to figure out exactly what was going on and be able to satisfy the auditors that the amounts were fairly stated on the Balance Sheet. The guy that had been doing the accounting was smart enough but had some difficulty with oral communications. As a result, management was highly suspicious of what was going on, as were the auditors. After working with him for a while, I figured out there was someone else who knew the operational details much better so off I went to get that valuable institutional knowledge.

I finally got to meet with him in person after a couple of postponements which got me thinking this would not be easy. We chatted for a bit and then I posed some direct questions about how things worked. It was when I was following up with more specific questions for clarification that he was getting uneasy. I could tell by his shuffling papers and moving about behind his desk. I had been through similar situations in the past and typically backed off because there was no real urgency. But in this case, the guy had already put me off a couple times, and there was no one else who knew what he did. So I pressed on. After all, this was my assignment to find out exactly what was going on and document it.

This is when he blew his stack. "Get out! Get out of my office! Now!" I wasn't getting paid enough to deal with a raving lunatic so I left. I felt like I was defeated and wasn't sure how I'd proceed. So I went to my boss, the Controller who hired me and told him what happened. He laughed! And evidently was not surprised at all and seemed happy that I was getting close to the root of the problem. I let the guy cool off for a few days and I think during that time he realized that he went too far. So, with the support of my boss, I set up another meeting and things went much better. I didn't get an apology but got the information I was after.

I worked at Washington Gas for about another year after that, at which point I got to thinking about another career move. Later in Chapter 5 I describe how the Audit Manager at Washington Gas Energy Services ended up with a federal government job. Well, I often thought about what that would be like. I had heard that the jobs were very secure and the benefits were great. Plus, I was a little worn out being the hired gun to solve problems that others couldn't. If I got a government job I was pretty sure it would be relatively easy; plus, since I hadn't yet vested in healthcare benefits it looked like just what I needed to cruise out into a real retirement.

Chapter 4 - What's Behind the Curtain

Hopefully everyone who reads this book has seen the movie or read "The Wizard of Oz." Remember when Dorothy accidentally got a peak behind the curtain and saw that the great and glorious Wizard was just an ordinary tubby old man? Throughout my career I always wondered what someone else's job was like. In college I had a friend who had a part-time (during school) and summer job at a General Motors plant on an assembly line making way more per hour than I ever did. How did he get a Union job like that? When I was able to afford my first home purchase my father-in-law knew a Realtor, and one afternoon we went looking at a few homes for sale and settled on one shortly afterward. At closing, when I saw the commission the Realtor earned, I couldn't believe someone could make so much money in such a short period of time. That played on my mind wondering what really went on behind that curtain, and I eventually took classes and got my Realtor's license.

The real estate classes were filled with future Realtors and me. I was really excited to meet these people and especially my teachers. I felt like I breeched the barrier and was close to finding out all the secrets of making easy money. I was doing this during the evenings in my spare time since I was working full time as an Accounting Manager at Columbia Energy. What made it really fun was the fact that the courses were actually interesting and the material to be tested on was pretty easy stuff like: how many square feet in an acre. The Realtor sponsoring the training was really nice and sort-of took me under his wing because he knew my potential based on my background in finance. He actually let me take the tests ahead of time and so I got my license pretty fast and was ready to sell sell sell! After the course, he and the Broker/Owner invited me to lunch and pitched coming to work for their firm. They knew that I held a full-time "real job" but wanted me anyway since I told them I was unhappy in my current position. It was a white lie, to make sure I could actually get inside a company as a full fledged Realtor.

I was so excited about my new license and when I got my business cards and a supply of monthly real estate newsletters with my picture on the front, I honestly thought I was on the verge of getting clients and making fat commissions. I would get up before sunrise on the weekends and go out to the apartments and condos in the area and hand deliver my sappy newsletter with real estate advice and cooking recipes. After doing that for weeks, I realized what a schmuck I was. I didn't get one call.

The full-time Realtors hated part-timers. It's no wonder since their living depended on it and the part-timers were there to cut into their territories. However, I was undaunted and forged ahead, trying to learn everything I could. Since I was part-time I ended up working some evenings and weekends. The full-time Realtors in our office liked handing off their listings to me for a weekend open house since they preferred working week days and open houses rarely produced a buyer; mostly just "lookie-loos." The main reason Realtors did them was to snag new buyers and show them other properties.

I remember one time, just to get the experience, I was offered a listing from one of the big producing Realtors for a Saturday open house. I had learned from the courses I took that it's always a good idea to preview the house so as to familiarize oneself with the layout etc. The office set up my preview; then I went to the house and nobody was there. Using the lockbox, I let myself in and starting looking around, familiarizing myself with the nuances like where the bathroom was. Who knows, I might get someone actually interested with a question or two. Then, while in the living room I saw it, an 8 x 12 picture of my bosses administrative assistant (secretaries in those days) was sitting on the piano. Immediately I recalled that she was moving; so yes, this was her house! Holy crap, none of the higher ups at the office knew I was moonlighting as a Realtor. And if it was found out that I was in her house, I'd come across as some sort of snooping pervert or a jerk at best.

So I scrammed out of there before anyone came home, and explained to the listing agent that I didn't want the open house after all, since the neighbor had this huge satellite dish in their front yard and I didn't think it would sell. Of course he gave me the old salesman's pitch about why it would sell and that I was crazy for not taking the open house. He was right of course, but I stood my ground; I had no choice. So I told him thanks but no thanks and walked away. I'm sure he was shaking his head.

I mentioned about Delaware being the small wonder in Chapter One. Another part of my Realtor training was shadowing one of the experienced Realtors on a listing presentation. This is where a Realtor goes out to the potential home seller and tells them what they want to hear about their house in the hopes of getting the homeowner to sign a listing agreement. My mentor Tucker introduced me to the son of the co-owner of the Real Estate Brokerage. Let's call him Bo. He was a legacy and resident hot shot around the office, good looking, smooth talker etc. He had his picture on billboards and in the real estate section of the newspaper all the time. And the ads that he would run would always have a funny stupid twist that set him apart from all the other Realtors.

Two of us newbies were lucky enough to tag along with him on a listing presentation that very evening. We went to a fairly upscale townhouse community and rang the bell. Well, who showed up but another woman from where I worked. She was a little surprised to see me but since she worked for a totally different department I wasn't too concerned about it getting out that I was doing real estate business on the side. So we all walked through her place with Bo leading the way. Walking past some book shelves he noticed a book he had read and mentioned to her how great he thought it was. She was impressed! Who knows whether he actually knew anything about the book, but he sure could schmooze.

She ended up signing the listing agreement that night. I was pretty sure that my credibility with her from work helped seal the deal but according to Bo it was all him. He showed us how it was done and let everyone at the office know it. He was good alright, but a little shady to say the least. I am pretty sure he sabotaged an advertisement I wanted to run for a listing I had. I eventually got him back though.

I was sitting at the bar one evening with a friend and in walks Bo with his buddies and sat at table. He didn't notice me and not sure he would have recognized me anyway. So after a couple drinks I convinced my friend to go over to Bo and act like he was in the market for buying a house, a big one. I saw Bo's eyes light up and I let it go on for a while before I made him aware of my little prank. I'm not sure he even knew what was going on but I did get a good laugh out of it.

Even though I sold a couple of homes, after about 6 months I had my fill. And it was time to go back concentrating on my real job. Selling real estate can be very lucrative, but you have to invest a lot of time, be able to sling the bull really well and put up with a lot of disappointments. Even though the sales commissions were high, the clients rarely fell right into your lap and there is nothing worse than investing a lot of time and money on a deal that goes sour at the end.

Chapter 5 - Hiring and Firing at the Federal Government

Landing a job at the federal government depends on who you are. What I mean is not exactly who you are but what you are. I didn't work in Human Resources but I experienced enough hiring situations to be fairly confident in what I'm writing. If one has the right attributes, you move to the top of the heap...yes, it's affirmative action at its finest!

Now, you may be wondering what affirmative action class I belong to. As it turns out, my military veteran status got me in the door. I sought a government job after hearing about a couple other former associates landing government jobs. Both of them, in my opinion were not exactly Einsteins when it came to finance and accounting; plus, they looked like me but were not veterans. So what was their "attribute" that got them in?

Manny was a former boss of mine actually. He just happened to interface with the Securities and Exchange Commission (SEC) point of contact (POC) as part of his job at the major utility company at which we were both employed. By interface I mean pretty much in name only. Correspondence went out with his name on it, even though it was developed by others, and incoming requests for information came to him since he was our POC. He basically coordinated the effort to reply. So, after years of doing this he built a casual working relationship with the SEC chief assigned to our company. Don't get me wrong, Manny wasn't a dummy and did get involved in formulating replies and making decisions but Manny's bosses were the drivers of any strategy and ultimate decision makers. Plus, any requests from the SEC and any responses to them were all in writing. When the company we worked for was bought out, Manny's past "experience" gave him the foot in the door at the SEC, one of the highest paying agencies in the government. It didn't hurt that, from the SEC standpoint, they were able to grab someone supposedly with "insider information." It also didn't hurt that Manny had a clean resume with a decent college GPA and, albeit brief, big accounting firm experience.

I remained friends with Manny and over the years he encouraged me to apply to the SEC or the federal government in general, but I was pretty sure that on paper I would not make it through the screening process. Plus, I really didn't need a better job at the time so inertia ruled the day.

The other guy that landed a government job was the audit Manager for Price Waterhouse Coopers (PWC) when I was consulting for Washington Gas. His attribute was big accounting firm experience; and a Manager too. Why wouldn't the government want someone like that? On paper, this guy must have had a high GPA just to get into that firm, and the mere fact that he was a manager shows his technical competence and managerial qualities, right? Maybe not.

You don't really rise above the ranks in a public accounting firm unless you make Partner. Managers are a dime a dozen and they come and go like used car salespeople. When we worked together at Washington Gas (WG), I was the consultant hired to dig into one of their subsidiary's books and basically validate their Balance Sheet. Yes, they had been audited but there were a few problem areas that needed to be cleaned up and reconciled. It was also management's thinking to possibly sell that line of business.

During my review I came upon a few areas of the Balance Sheet that were unreconciled and/ needed more support. For example if you show a balance in Accounts Receivable for $1,000, you should have copies of the unpaid invoices adding up to the $1,000. I hope this is not getting too technical. Think of it as a loan application for a mortgage and the mortgagee requesting documentation of the assets you provided to them in your application. If you don't have the support it may be viewed as fraud.

Well, when I asked the subsidiary financial management to give me the supporting documentation, they referred me to the auditors. That's right; they did not have the support and had relied on the auditors to reconcile and verify the support. That was my first clue that I was in for some interesting forensic challenges.

Now back to the whole point about the audit manager. When I went to the auditors to get the support supposedly available, they shared with me the analysis of Accounts Receivable A/R. It consisted of a "roll-forward" of the A/R balance from one period to the next. That was all they were doing. They spent time verifying the activity from last year to this year but did not have supporting invoices that reconciled to the outstanding balance. Well, to make a long story short, when the audit Partner found out that the Manager and his staff were not able to substantiate the balances in certain General Ledger accounts I could tell by his "deer in the headlights" look, that he was livid. A couple months later a new audit manager showed up and I found out that the prior manager had left, but found a job with the federal government…very interesting.

The two examples above don't fit into the affirmative action hiring approach I led off with, but they do reinforce a couple of other points I'm trying to make in this book. One, people sometimes escape from private industry to find a cushier job in the public sector; and two, the government doesn't do much research into one's former occupational experience as long as you check certain boxes in the application process.

When I would hire an accountant in the private sector we had a Human Resources (HR) department that actually had an interest in getting the best candidate hired for the position. They would do the advertising based on input from the hiring authority and screen the candidates not only on paper but bring them in for a face to face interview. That process usually resulted in the hiring authority getting to interview a small handful of the top candidates based on the HR screening process. It generally worked out very well, primarily since the HR department took the time to learn what I was looking for and was sincerely working to help select the best candidate to fill the position.

At the VA, I was responsible for hiring financial management accountants but given very little leeway on who gets hired. The basic process was as follows:

After justifying the need to fill a vacancy the requisition is turned over to HR where it disappears into a black hole for weeks. Typically, the position to be filled is advertised both within the government and outside the government as well. There was an option to fill a vacancy from within but since the existing population of government candidates were deemed to be mediocre (and justifiably so, see Chapter 8), the search usually went outside the government as well.

Once the position opening was posted it would be at least a couple months before resumes were available to review. This was not because HR was doing due diligence in screening the applicants. It was because they were taking their time seeing how many points to award each applicant based on their secret criteria. They would not disclose this process but it was pretty obvious what happened once the stacks of applications were available for review. We never knew how many applications were tossed in the trash, but it was curious why better quality applicants never seemed to make it through, especially since the job openings averaged about $60,000 -$80,000 per year salary and I had first hand knowledge of people that would apply and never make it through the HR screening.

What we did end up getting is usually the same stack of internal candidates that were perennial job seekers, leftovers that no other agency or department really wanted. Before retiring from my Director's position I was charged with finding my replacement. After several rounds of interviews, even the best ones rated by our panel would have such a bad reputation that our Senior Management would nix the selection as soon as they heard the candidate's name. The truly good candidates were typically retained by their own agency and promoted to higher levels, and there were many levels.

By now you are probably wondering...how did I make it through?

Chapter 6 - I Got a Government Job!

Joining the Army Reserve Officers Training Corps (ROTC) in college was one of the best decisions I ever made. The benefits have been enormous: $100 a month while I was in college (actually worth something in the 70's); a student deferment during while the lottery draft was still in effect; serving as an officer in the Army vs. enlisting as a private; and I'm pretty damn sure it got my foot in the door for a job at the Department of Veterans Affairs.

As I mentioned before, there is a secret list of preference items and criteria used by HR to screen candidates for jobs. One criterion not able to be kept secret is Veteran Status. In fact, during the last few years of my service at the VA, it was so heavily weighted towards veterans both in terms of hiring and contracting we could not, as a practical matter, hire anyone but a veteran. It was so blatantly obvious that when we finally received a stack of applications for a vacancy, the veterans were at the top of the stack with the "most qualified" box checked. It was HR's way of telling us who to select.

Now being a veteran myself and knowing many smart and well qualified veterans from my Finance Officers Basic class and subsequent work experience, I did not have any problem at all with hiring a qualified veteran. What I did have a problem with is hiring a veteran without the requisite training and experience needed to do the job. I recall one instance where our selection panel interviewed one of the "most qualified" veterans. We set up an initial phone interview 9 am. Shortly after the interview started, the candidate asked us to "hold on; I'm going into an elevator". He was actually interviewing while driving/walking on his way to work…unbelievable. Other veteran candidates were deemed "most qualified" by HR by mentioning the words accounting or finance in their resume. Again, these jobs typically paid $60,000 - $80,000 or more for a degreed Accountant with experience. This is one of the many ways the government would be willing to spend money without accountability (see Chapter 11 for more on that).

Looking back now, my application to the VA must have been viewed as golden since not only was I a veteran, I actually had a high degree of relevant experience. When I first received a call for an interview it was about two months after submitting my application online. The first interview was a phone interview with a panel doing round robin questions. I hardly prepared for the interview since I thought there was only a slim chance of getting the job. However, I felt I did reasonably well considering there are definitely some significant differences between accounting for a federal government entity vs. one in the private sector. The main difference was the system of budgetary accounting in federal government. The private sector had budgeting but nowhere near the level of complexity and breath of a government budget operation.

When I was asked by my future boss about the differences I sort of bluffed my way through it. I was guessing that there were more similarities than actual differences between the two and as it turns out, I was right! So I played toward my strengths and about a month later got a call for an in-person interview. If you're counting, yes, it was three months so far.

In the interview I was fortunate enough to connect well with my future boss. I remember seeing an old blue intermediate accounting book on his bookshelf and asked him if that was the same text book I used in college by Welsch, Zlatkovich and White. If he only knew that I knew very little about what was inside the book but had memorized the authors' names by just starring at the outside cover during classes I actually attended. He was about the same age as me and the line of questioning was more social than technical. And I think I clinched the interview when his boss saw that I went to the University of Delaware. His daughter had recently decided that's where she wanted to go to college. So I went along and said what a good school it was. A little white lie never hurt anyone.

I honestly expected my first days on the job to be filled with orientations, training and coffee breaks. However, after being shown my cubicle and being introduced to my fellow staff members, I was actually put to work. Was this the government job I had led myself to believe was a cake walk? I dug in and put my best effort into absorbing all I could so as to not look like I was a hiring mistake. To make matters worse, my information technology skills had not been honed as of late since I was mostly managing others for the previous 25 years. So when it came to working with the VA's antiquated financial management system (the general ledger (GL) guts), combined with a new reporting system they had recently adopted to interface with the GL system to say I was overwhelmed is an understatement. To extract information from the GL system it was like I was back in the 1970s trying to write strings of programming language that only machines could understand. And coming into the organization at a fairly senior level I was expected to either know this stuff already or catch on rapidly.

It wasn't until about a month later that I began to realize that those pressures were all in my mind. It really WAS the federal government, and soon I was working circles around my co-workers and being recognized by management. I always had a good work ethic so it was natural for me to work diligently and even voluntarily worked overtime (mostly because we got compensatory time off and I had not built up any vacation time yet). It was easy asking questions once I got to know the people around me and most, but not all, were helpful. As is typical, the ones most helpful were the ones either confident in their abilities or those so lost they just wanted to be nice. The ones most difficult were those afraid someone would "find them out" or felt threatened by me professionally.

A recurring theme of this book is how overpaid and useless most government workers are. Now don't turn this into "all government workers", just MOST. It was fairly well known by my peers that the 80/20 rule was in effect across all the financial management personnel in the federal government. That meant that 20 percent of the personnel did 80 percent of the work. The rest of the personnel were either retired on the job or clueless in their performance. In fact, if you gave actual work to many of these folks, you were just asking for more trouble from the mistakes they would make. They were, to a large extent counter-productive. That's why the 20 percent would do most the work.

Chapter 7 - Assuming the Directorship

One of the most irritating things about working in an accounting department is deadlines. To meet the deadlines and provide a decent work product, your unit has to be staffed appropriately, both in terms of: 1) experience/proficiency; and 2) the number of bodies to get the job done. Although fairly simple in concept, it is not understood the higher up you go in the organization. Most accounting departments are viewed as "bean counters" by higher-ups, and, as a general rule, you never get the respect in terms of adequate resources to accomplish your mission.

Turnover in the accounting department is a killer. And the federal government is set up to keep employees constantly bouncing around, whether it's to another office in the same agency or, to another agency/department. Once your job gets a little uncomfortable there is generally another opening readily available, sometimes multiple ones if you're willing to move laterally or even down a grade. I was recently reviewing applicants for our never ending revolving door and noticed one of them was actually working in a position that was a grade lower than he had been working months before. In the private sector, that would have been an indication of a demotion, or someone to be leery of. But my fellow interview panelists told me that was not unusual. In fact one of my future bosses said, "I did that...just to get out; it's done all the time."

You can imagine how often that would happen in a unit that has never ending deadlines…combined with a couple bosses (like me for instance) that feel responsible for producing a decent work product. The funny thing is, though, that most of those that have left the VA end up coming back or wanting to come back eventually (even a couple back to my section).

Here's an example of what I mean about the government permitting job-hopping. This time it's me. The VA Finance Director who hired me eventually left his position to work with his former boss who had been reassigned not too long after I was hired. Why this took so long (after "she"[3] came on board) I'll never know. Since he was a really smart government accounting technician and all-around good guy I knew I too had to get out. It could only get worse without him there to run interference and absorb the body blows from the new executive.

So I applied for a lateral assignment in the Veteran's Health Administration (VHA), a division of the VA known for being so big that getting things done fast was never a realistic objective. Plus they had a finance executive team that actually cared about their employees well-being. Landing that job took longer than expected, mostly because I failed to submit the magic SF-52 form (an innocuous status form that HR maintains) with my application and that got my application trashed right away. Forget the fact that I was

---

[3] "She" refers to the Associate that the Deputy Assistant Secretary for Finance brought on board from the Department of Defense in a mini management shake-up. She was to eventually become my boss.

most qualified and the SF-52 document was a standard form that HR has a record of anyway. I got trapped by not knowing how the system works because it was the first time I actually applied for another position since starting with the VA five years prior. That period of time without applying for another job may actually be a record for federal employees. So, when the VHA hiring authority realized I didn't make the cut, he did the only thing left…re-advertised the position! HR doesn't really care that you do that. They would rather waste time and go through the whole process again, than simply pull a form they had on file.

By the way, I did appeal the HR action of excluding me, all the way to an HR executive. They couldn't grant an exception, even though the application form was not clear about the SF-52. She (the HR executive I challenged), by the way, was eventually reassigned due to her role in the HR conference spending scandal of 2012. You may have read about that one in the newspapers (if not, Google it). It's the one where they paid an actor thousands of dollars to dress as General George Patton and make a short movie speech to rally the HR troops. The making of the video cost $52,000.

So, back to the point about job-hopping made easy. Not only did I make the list the second time around, I got the job (the fix was in anyway). And that's only half the story. No sooner did my bosses boss (I'll call him Mr. Ed) find out about it, than in came my new boss almost begging me to stay. It was a pitiful sight to behold. So, without having actually started my new VHA position, I applied for my former boss's job, the Director position. As is true even in the private sector, even when the fix is in, you still need to go through the make-believe process of advertising, interviewing etc. Needless to say, I got the job. Truthfully, I didn't really want the Director's job but I like more money and I was told that I would not be held accountable for the ineptness of my staff members, most of whom at the time, should not have been in an accounting department. So there you go...I had three different jobs in the span of a month or so...completely legit from an HR perspective.

Chapter 8 - My Cracker Jack Staff

I remember early in my tenure when we had a change in management and the woman that took over our financial reporting section was soliciting feedback from an assembly of our entire staff. It was sort of an informal survey of the attitudes of the staff during the transition. One of the informal leaders of the group responded that she was a member of the KMA club. I found out later what she meant was since she was vested in retirement, she now belonged (as did many) to the Kiss My Ass club. This particular individual ended up reporting to me and I got to know how that club operated first hand. She would often be late for work, use up all sick leave accrued, and when asked to do work would disappear for hours. I gave up on trying to motivate her but eventually hired someone else to supervise her and some of the others in that club. It helped to build a record of behavior, and once they figured out we were going to start holding them accountable, they started to actually retire…for real.

I could fill another book of anecdotes about highly paid accountant/analyst types that most people would find unbelievable. Following are a just few examples of the most bone headed cases:

A woman (let's call her Amy) was getting about $100,000 as a Grade 13 Accountant. Her problem was adding up numbers. Schedules prepared by her were submitted for review without even being correctly footed (accounting term for correctly adding down and across). Sounds crazy, doesn't it? After seeing this was getting to be a habit, I confronted her about checking her work before turning it in. Her response to me was "I thought that's what YOU were supposed to do". It turns out none of her work was to be trusted and we should not have given her any work to do; it would have saved us countless hours of figuring out problems caused by her mistakes. Eventually she was placed on a Performance Improvement Plan (PIP) but before that played out she knew where it was headed and managed to find a job with another department known for its ineptness.

Chatty was an Analyst. A well paid position with a greater breath of responsibility and flexibility of assignment. She was a very long tenured employee (member of the KMA club) and was our liaison with HR and and other external matters such as the auditors. We had just expended a lot of effort meeting a target date for a financial report to be reviewed by the external auditors, and very proud of meeting the date. This was turned over to Chatty to send to the auditors asap. The next day my boss at the time told me the auditors were asking for our report. I have to say I was more than a little concerned so I went to Chatty's office, sat down, and tried to find out what happened. I was not getting a straight answer so I stood up and closed her office door since I did not feel that the little reprimand I was about to discharge should be heard by others. At least that's how I was trained as a manager. If done in private with a cooperative spirit a ver-bal reprimand would have a better chance of changing behavior.

As I was closing the door she loudly exclaimed "don't you shut that door!" I was totally surprised by that reaction and tried to explain my reason for wanting to shut the door. She kept repeating "don't shut the door" until a few people started to congregate, one of which was my boss. So, I explained the situation and left. At least then I knew there's another one not to trust with anything important.

Joy was our Admin. Assistant. She was another member of the KMA club. She was bigger than most everyone else and mean looking to boot. So, it's no wonder nobody held her accountable for the many years it took to make it to the club. One day I gave her a binder of information to be copied. She could either do it herself or send it to the duplicating department. I told her it was no particular rush. I knew she would not like doing that so I thought giving her plenty of time would make it easier for her. Well, who would have suspected that not only was the job not done after a week's time, but when I asked her about it she told me it was lost. Yes, that's right. It was gone. And since she didn't report to me directly there was nothing much I could do about it. Her superior was well aware of the Joy problem and was evidently not able or willing to do anything about it. So Joy succeeded in getting very few assignments from me or anyone else. I think she may still be on the job spending your hard-earned tax money...and mine!

Oh, here's another Joy classic. I sent her an e-mail on a Saturday when my accounting staff was working overtime to meet a Treasury deadline. After not hearing back from her by late on Monday, or maybe it was Tuesday, I called her to see why she had not responded. Her answer was that since she doesn't work the weekends, she didn't get my e-mail. Another one for the "one of a kind" file.

Jane was another shining example of how in the hell did she end up in financial management. And if you're reading this thinking I'm a sexist by now, it's not true. It's just that most of the existing staff I inherited when named Director were women. There were plenty of guys at the VA who screwed things up as well and got paid handsomely for doing it. Jane was another member of the KMA club but you wouldn't know it by her attitude. She was a genuinely nice person and often stopped by to encourage me early on when I was new to the Department. I found out later that she was "protected." I'm not sure of the details but evidently she had filed a claim against the VA in the past and was transferred into this unit and basically assigned very little. When she formally reported to me I had been around long enough to know the situation. I could not easily figure out what value she added to our section so one day I asked her to document the process she used to complete a particular assignment. That was pretty much all that it took to get her to start her retirement paperwork. Don't get me wrong…I was not some ogre or task master, or was I? Was I creating a hostile work environment by trying to get staff members to actually do productive work, and correctly? Some think I was.

When I took over the Director's position everyone was pretty happy at first. As a GS - 14 senior staff accountant, I was everyone's friend. I helped them out here and there and just wanted to fit in and not rock the (gravy) boat. The Director I replaced (Jim Bob) was very knowledgeable in government accounting, well-liked by everyone and had the patience of a saint. Jim Bob knew I was a valuable employee and would aways look out for me and give me the benefit of the doubt in every situation...except one. Whenever I even remotely brought up the notion of how on earth he doesn't lose his temper or even raise his voice or complain, he just changed the subject. I still wonder about how he ended up with such a bunch of misfits. The only conclusion I could reach is that because the government, as a practical matter could never fire anyone, maybe the problem cases were funneled to the only guy who could deal with such incompetence without blowing a gasket. Everyone makes hiring mistakes, including myself, but that was just too many to believe.

I took the Director's position as previously described in Chapter 7. I didn't really want it but was faced with the possibility of having a new boss and either being expected to carry the workload of the whole section (actually me and one other staff person I'll get to in chapter 9) for the same paycheck. And besides I was told by more than one person that the best job in government is a non-supervisory GS-14. Later I would appreciate how true that statement was.

My management style was very no-nonsense. I worked pretty hard, setting an example, and felt that everyone else should at least try to do the same. Some call it a Type A management style or personality. It's part of my inner make-up; some things people just can't change. It's actually a curse. When faced with a problem I tackle it head on, try to do the right thing and in the most efficient way; and in doing so may come across as a jerk. This goes way back to one of my first leadership roles.

As mentioned earlier I was in ROTC in college. Between my Junior and Senior year, during basic training at Fort Bragg in North Carolina, we took turns being platoon leader. When it was my turn, I acted like I was in charge…oops! There were a couple of goof-offs that didn't want to be there in the first place and all the marching around and saluting was beneath them. They were certainly a little miffed when I called them on their undisciplined behavior. After all, who was this jerk who is no better than us telling us what to do? They made jokes about it and obviously several others fell in right there with them because when the peer ratings came out at the end of training I was way down on the list.

It was a little bit of a blow to my ego, but I knew I was pretty good at the military business anyway. I had played war[4] since I was a little kid; I won the Freshman ROTC class competition for assembly and disassembly of the M1 A1 rifle; and was the only cadet out of our entire Junior class that received a "spot report" after basic training that summer. It was awarded by the "real army" folks at Ft. Bragg based on my performance in a practice reconnaissance mission where my squad snuck up on and captured real Army members of the 82nd Airborne Division. Our real Army Captain at the University had told us that these reports are rarely ever given out. And he told us this before the training so I know it wasn't just BS.

---

[4]Playing war consisted of my friends and I dividing into two teams, arming ourselves with fake civil war era muskets and basically playing hide and seek in the woods. Since caps for cap guns cost money we would usually get by with just saying "dow dow dow" to simulate firing shots. Kind of like playing paintball without the paintballs.

I tucked this episode with the peer reports away and used it as a learning experience. Later on in my career, when faced with a new leadership challenge, I would think back to what happened and take it slow…real slow. Ultimately, however, one has to deal with the bad eggs and it wasn't too long before I got a reputation in some circles at the VA as possibly creating a hostile work environment. Fortunately I knew deep down the few complaints weren't justified so I didn't let it bother me, even when my boss subtly brought up her past experience where "someone she knew" in the past had caught some real trouble for that.

At first, "Jay" was the only other male on staff early in my Directorship. He was a really nice guy but very young, inexperienced and frankly, a little lazy. I remember working with Jay on intra-governmental (I-Gov) accounting issues. The VA did a lot of business with other agencies like the Department of Defense (DOD), Department of Labor (DOL), etc. The idea was to make sure that the transactions with affiliates were recorded at the same time and for the same amounts so things would always be in balance. Pretty simple, right? But put the transactions in the hands of typical government employees and chances are -0- that things would balance. In fact these transactions across the government were constantly out of balance by millions and sometimes billions of dollars (see Chapter X for more on I-Gov accounting). One day while working with Jay as we were closing the books at quarter end I got into the detailed process he was using to provide Treasury the VA side of these transactions. This was a manual process, in part because the VA's General Ledger as well as most of the larger agencies' and departments' ledgers were not capable of providing the correct information in the same format without manual adjustments.

So I would ask Jay how he arrived at VA's balances and he said it depends. If comparing VA's balance to the Department of Defense (DoD's), Jay would supply Treasury VA's own actual balances since the DoD was messed up way more than the VA's books. DoD would then use VA's balance to adjust to because they knew and agreed that DoD accounting was probably not correct. If it was the Department of Labor (DOL) that VA was being compared to and there was a large imbalance between the two, Jay would manually adjust VA's balance to agree to DOL because VA was never confident in how to record transactions with DOL.

The VA got away with that approach for quite some time until Treasury, who put together the financial statements for the entire federal government as a whole decided to implement a new system for gathering financial information from all of the Agencies and Departments. This went into effect around 2015 and basically exposed all of the weaknesses and cover-ups in intra-governmental accounting. What a mess that was, but if the Treasury was ever expected to get an audit opinion on the federal government's financial statements they had to start fixing things and sometimes you need to take a couple of steps backward before making progress. The funny thing about their quest to get a valid audit opinion was they would never, ever really get there as a practical matter. This was because the most significant liabilities of the federal government could never be captured even using estimates. It's a constantly moving target, changing day to day based on hundreds, if not thousands of external forces, political and otherwise. See Chapter 10 for a discussion about government financial reporting and why billions of dollars are being wasted in an attempt to report financial statements of the government like the private sector does. One of the main points I'm trying to drive home in this book is "accounting vs. accountability." They are NOT the same and the federal government needs the later, not the former.

After I passed Jay over for a promotion opportunity, he left the VA looking for greener pastures. Several months later he was calling me back saying it was a mistake to leave the VA…oh well. That happened a lot at the VA; Out of the frying pan and into the fire (except back then nobody in the federal government ever got fried, let alone fired).

Ginny was another original staff member and then a subordinate of mine. She was not in the KMA club but was always taking time off for one reason or another. As soon as she accrued a day or two of leave, she would leave. My favorite story about her was just before noon on one beautiful sunny day, she comes to me requesting sick leave for the rest of the day. I probably should not have asked why but my curiosity was getting the best of me as she seemed perfectly fine. So after I asked, she thought for a moment and then blurted out "stomach ache". I said okay, I hope you feel better. About an hour later, I see her coming up the stairwell with a big plate of food from the cafeteria. Maybe her illness was just hunger pains.

These are all true stories. And remember, these are just examples, a handful of the direct experiences I've had with ordinary government employees. And for every example I write about there are hundreds and maybe thousands more I experienced over my 10 years at the VA.

I could go on and on with these types of stories but I think I've made my point. The 80/20 rule within VA's financial management was no exaggeration. What made it even worse, besides being so unfair to the 20 percent actually performing, was that the 80% were drawing large salaries paycheck after paycheck without fear of losing their job when I knew so many in the private sector making far less without the job security and benefits. And to top it off, the federal income taxes being paid by those in the private sector are subsidizing the salaries of those under-performing federal employees. In my way of thinking it's almost like stealing if the non-performing personnel are not being held accountable.

Karen was another staff accountant with issues. Being an accounting operation, our workload is bunched around closing deadlines mostly set by the Treasury Department. A closing schedule is disseminated to all involved so everyone knows how to plan their personal leave. Not only is it important to be on the job during these crunch periods, it also typically involves some overtime, so it's not very pleasant.

So every quarter I would get "special requests" for time off during the critical closing periods. For most of 30 years prior to coming to the VA I sacrificed my personal life to be at work for quarterly and year-end closings. And in the Army we were told that the only excuse for missing an important exercise was "a death in the family - namely YOUR OWN." Needless to say, one had to be cordial in denying most of the requests; can't create a hostile work environment! It did rub me the wrong way, though, when I got these requests. Everyone knew the block-out periods well in advance but would still test me, maybe to see if I would snap and then they'd file a claim of harassment.

Since the closing schedules were in writing, most of the staff did end up being at work when expected… except for Karen. One year-end she missed most of closing due to migraines etc. I couldn't pry too much unless there was a certain number of days in a row missed, in which case one would need a doctor's note. But a good government employee knows all those rules and how to get around them.

The most egregious case was when I denied Karen's request to go on leave during the time Treasury needed a quick turn-around on their draft government-wide financial report. This was all documented in writing but still she decided to really put me to the test and just not show up for work. It really wasn't fair to the other staff members who did show up and I was not about to just let it go. So I had to set an example and, after much consultation with management and HR, gave her a written reprimand. She was shocked to get it and tried to appeal. That turned out to be futile because of the written record of e-mails documenting our correspondence. Surprisingly enough, even Human Resources totally supported me in that effort since the undeniable evidence of her insubordination was handed to them earlier.

Since the turnover in our section was pretty steady, I had to hire new Accountants and Analysts fairly regularly. One such hire was a guy I thought would add value to our unit.

Ronnie was very experienced in government accounting and convinced me in the interview that he knew more than just the basics of budgetary accounting. That was a rare find due to it's (unnecessary) complexity. As previously covered in Chapter 5, it was very difficult to find really good candidates internally and the good ones from outside the government seemed to be usually screened out by HR.

Ronnie had even offered his current supervisor as a reference. Whon I finally reached out to her, she was confused. And the reason for that was she didn't even know Ronnie was looking for another job! I think I caught her by surprise and to this day I'll never know if her positive recommendation was sincere or she was just thankful to get rid of him. As it turns out Ronnie was so experienced, he knew the ropes, so to speak. He mastered the art of the "hide and slide" technique. After a while I got the impression he was on cruise control, keeping a low profile and counting the days until retirement. I remember getting comments from my superiors about Donnie's apparent shyness, since he would rarely make eye contact with someone in the hallways. And pretty much everything I said to Ronnie was followed by him responding "yes sir!" He said it every time so I couldn't tell if he was being genuine or sarcastic.

Another tell of his jaded disposition was when I would challenge something he did, and I would even be nice about it so as not to get him even more upset than he normally was. I recall a meeting where my staff got together to discuss a financial reporting issue where a number on one page in the report would not always tie to a similar number elsewhere in the report, mostly due to rounding of the number either up or down. And occasionally a schedule would not add down and across, being off by rounding as well. Ronnie commented that if it's just rounding we should not be concerned. When I explained that any financial report I've ever been associated with always needed to be perfectly footed and cross-referenced he responded "Yes sir; I'll never bring up ideas like that again!" It reminded me of a teacher's comment that I received on a third grade report card stating "does not accept criticism well". Ronnie knew that his demeanor would spread the message for everyone to leave him alone. And they did.

The above examples were blunders of my subordinates and some of my peers. I could write another book on the goofs/poor judgment of my superiors but I'll just mention a few so you get the flavor of what went on.

Midway through my Directorship tenure my second boss Katie was able to convince management to fill the vacancy she had for a Deputy. We'll call him DD, short for Deputy Dog, the cartoon character. DD had some fairly extensive government experience for what that's worth but I don't think he had much experience managing people. Katie did tell me that she wanted me to apply for her Deputy position but little did she know that it was difficult enough for me to minimize the time spent with her let alone serving as her Deputy. To set the stage for this story one has to appreciate the scope of my responsibilities. The Director of Management and Financial Reports Service played a central role in consolidating all the financial information within the Department which was larger that many Fortune 500 companies in the private sector. I was a key liaison to senior management, the external auditors, the Inspector General's Office, the Office of Management and Budgets

(OMB), Treasury, and a host of other finance and accounting personnel across VA's wide network of operation. In addition to routine monthly and quarterly reporting we produced the annual Performance and Accountability Report (PAR), later split up between the Annual Financial Report and the budget focused Performance Report.

The underlying financial data of the statements ultimately produced was enormous. A couple times the auditors had requested a print-out of the entire general ledger containing all accounts. The Information Technology folks had to explain that what they were asking for would fill the hull of an aircraft carrier (a slight exaggeration, but they got the point). I was closest to the process of putting this all together into financial statements and honestly I was only able to analyze the information from a high level and had to rely on many others, deeper in the organization, for comfort on what was actually going on. So, it's no wonder that my immediate boss at the time, Senior Executive Service (SES) Katie, wanted someone else to ease her mind that the financial statements were fairly stated. So as not to piss me off, she told me that her Deputy would be primarily working on other matters, not financial reporting, but I knew why he was there. And it would not have bothered me as much if she was up front about it.

Since there was so much information contained in the financial statements the best way to get comfortable that newly produced statements were fairly correct was to analyze and explain the changes since the last audited set of financial statements. This basic concept used by preparers and auditors is a financial statement line item variation analysis. Some call it "analytics". When done properly the change in a line item, for example Revenue, is explained by using both quantitative and qualitative measures. Not only are changes in price and units taken into account (a rate/volume variation analysis) but an explanation of why those factors changed during the period in question is always integral to a good explanation. Plus, the explanation has to address a significant portion of the change, say 90%, to be considered valid.

I had been leading the effort to do that for a couple years and quite successfully I might add. Even the Office of Management and Budget (OMB) commented that VA's financial statement analysis was very good.

When DD came on board and saw what we were doing, he told us that a set of analytics going back 10 years would be better. That way, trends in the financial data over time could be discerned. I started to feel the temperature in my forehead rise. We are typically under the gun to produce the analytics, both for management and the auditors each quarter. And it was so difficult getting good explanations from the Administrations (the subsidiary units within the VA) that expanding the process would have a great cost without a practical benefit.

I tried to explain that to DD but he was not buying it. I think it was because he was new and wanted to exert his authority, not realizing there would have been other ways that made more sense. I think he was told that I reported to him and my boss had told me I would continue to report to her. It made for a very awkward situation. Since we were both a competitive sort neither one of us wanted to back down. He even went as far to tell me that he WILL get his way, one way or the other. And he did.

I found out later that he went around me to one of my staff members and that was not the first time. I think he was used to working with difficult people in the past and had assumed that I was one of them. Little did he know that my staff was pretty damn loyal to me and told me about it. So we worked out a little compromise. We would set up a spreadsheet that did comparisons for the last five years, not ten; and he agreed that was sufficient for the time being. It was rather useless because even though we eventually had the numbers all loaded in, the analysis was not. The first time we presented the huge spreadsheet for his review he realized that he didn't have enough time to absorb it all before we had to close the books. But stubborn as he was, he still wanted to see it. In the briefing meetings we had it was always funny to see his eyes shifting back and forth across that big spreadsheet looking for meaningless trends when what was really needed was to know what caused the changes since the last period which had been audited.

As previously mentioned we always had problems getting decent explanations from the larger subsidiary units of the VA (the Administrations). We constantly had to remind them we needed the business or economic reasons behind the change for a financial statement line item. Instead, they typically gave us a list of the component changes without the reasons for changes. For example, if the Veterans Benefits Administration had an increase in Veterans Benefits, they would tell us that the number of veterans receiving benefits went up and the average benefits cost went up, but would not provide the reasons why. And we felt fortunate to even get that. There were a lot of significant changes without any explanation at all, at least none that made sense. My staff and I became experts in spinning gold out of the straw we received in order to provide decent high-level analysis to management, OMB and others.

After a while, when the analysis really broke down because of all the focus on corrective action plans[5], the auditors would have a field day, writing us up for the lack of timely and accurate financial statement variation analysis. It took us a couple years to convince them that the root cause of this was at the Administration level, mostly the result of decentralized financial management[6]. Even worse was that our own financial management (central office in Washington DC) needed proof of the inadequate analysis we received from the Administrations. So we ended up having to supply detail of the timing of and inadequacy of analysis received…analysis of the analysis!

We had to turn over all this analysis to management and when DD found out that we hadn't been giving the auditors the five year spreadsheets, he blew a cork. He still didn't get the fact that trends in a balance over the last five or ten years were virtually useless in being able to explain current period changes, especially if we only had a few days to do it.

---

[5] Chapter 16 explains the workload increases brought about by a Senior Management change.

[6] See the Auditors Report in the Annual Financial Report of the VA for 2017 and 2018; also see Chapter 19.

It was about a year before I retired that DD and I started to get along much better. He had been taking quite a beating from our new senior management and he was realizing that even though the VA had many deep-seated financial management and reporting issues, I had been holding things together pretty well for years. And when he found out I was actually going to retire, he was the one that recommended an incentive payment for me to stick around for a while.

Chapter 9 - Sneaky Management

It is not my intention to trash the federal workforce at large. There are many good and necessary functions of government and lots of federal employees are true to their mission and genuinely try to do a good job. The worst problem I see is how the government allocates its resources and the pervasive culture that has developed because of the lack of backbone and the attitude of those in power not wanting to rock the boat. This is at the highest levels and most likely throughout the Senior Executive Service of all Agencies and Departments. Those at the senior levels rarely know exactly what is going on at the lower levels and avoid confrontation like the plague.

At the VA it was amazing to me to see how fearful management was of a potential lawsuit, yet the number of lawsuits were many. It's likely that the VA was often caught in a loop of settling lawsuits which led to more lawsuits and more settlements…on and on.

If a personnel conflict arose, the burden of proof was often on management before an action against an employee was enforced. The HR department was involved and so were the lawyers. An iron clad case had to be established before the most basic action, such as a letter of reprimand was issued. Management was very reluctant to hold a sub-par performer accountable because of the risk of retribution, plus it took a lot of time to document and participate in discussions that would have been necessary to prompt a change in the behavior of a problem employee or initiate an action to reprimand or dismiss an employee. At one point I was advised to secure at my own expense an umbrella insurance policy that would protect me against such a possibility of retribution. I never did because I truly felt that I not only acted properly at all times but would have the support of others familiar with my job performance.

That was a little naive on my part since, for various reasons, co workers are not necessarily as loyal as one might expect and telling the truth can't be relied upon. I've found that people often times make a judgment about someone without really knowing that person well or what the facts and circumstances are. I once criticized a consultant a few times directly since I felt that these professionals should be held to a higher standard than our regular employees. This was because they were not only viewed as being more knowledgeable in certain areas, but they were paid a lot more. She quit and shortly after I was told by my boss that I was the reason she quit. I should have received a bonus for that but instead I was viewed with skepticism. When, through my actions, people start leaving the department, some started to think that I was creating a hostile work environment rather that simply taking an honest view of someones performance and managing accordingly. Rewarding good performance and taking steps to deal with poor performance appropriately was not that easy.

Mary was our lead, most experienced Accountant in the VA Central Office Financial Reporting section. She was a good solid performer but worked very independently. By that I mean she "held the keys" to the books. As turnover occurred, as it normally does in a financial reporting department with deadlines, it's very important for procedures to be documented and a lot of cross-training to occur. Plus, when you add the fact that this was a federal government group of employees with plenty of sick leave and vacation time, it was a must to have clear documentation of procedures and trained back-up personnel for all critical job assignments.

It was somewhat challenging to get Mary to take what she knew and put it in writing or depart to someone else as a cross-training exercise. In fact, when I joined the department, documentation of procedures and journal entries was very scarce; it was almost nonexistent. I won't get too technical but one primary duty of central office Accountants is to put together the VA top level financial statements. In doing so, many "journal" entries are needed to eliminate transactions between units within the VA and to make adjusting entries for all sorts of reasons including correction of errors made at lower levels in the vast VA organization. Well, virtually none of the existing entries being made were documented as they should have been.

When I saw this, I couldn't really believe it but after seeing more and more journal entries with little support, I finally realized how bad the situation was. Very early in my career I was warned that if I ever got into a responsible accounting position where the books were a real mess I should get out right away. However, since this was only a Senior Staff position (GS-14) and I didn't yet have direct responsibility for statements, records, or people, I stuck around. I had to see how they were getting by...even with the auditors. And I knew that my job was pretty secure since there was so much needing attention.

But in order to fix things, you need to know how the underlying business operated and why transactions were being done the way they were. To make matters worse there was much guidance formally issued by Treasury for all Departments and Agencies to adhere to but it was mostly written in government-speak, not plain English. Try googling accounting for "distributed offsetting receipts" in the Treasury Financial Manual. You'll see what I mean.

It would take years to put together the puzzle pieces and not even then would the VA's financial reporting be anywhere near in compliance with all the regulations and guidance. But they had an unqualified "clean" opinion from the auditors! In actuality, however, the clean audit opinion is not so clean. If you look up the VA Annual Financial Report and read through the Auditor's Report, you'll start to wonder what an "unclean" report would look like. I'm pretty sure by now the VA financial management has gotten away from using the expression "clean" to describe their audit report.

In any event, I wanted to tell a little story that brings together my points about overly generous government time-off, the priority on formalized "training" and the sneaky underhanded way management at the VA sometimes operated.

Shortly after I had assumed the Directors role at the VA Central Office financial reporting section, I was coordinating an audit checklist that apparently had not been completed properly for years. It was nearing year-end and we were running out of time to complete this in time for the auditors to review. As previously mentioned, Mary had the most institutional knowledge needed to complete these checklist questionnaires. But, of course, she was not available since she was on "training" offsite with other financial management personnel. Because of my desire to actually make things happen on time I decided to exert my authority and set up a conference call so she could contribute to actual work getting accomplished as opposed to theoretical improvements by training. I was with my counterpart from Policy (we'll call him Jess) on a speakerphone and so was Mary as was normally done when dealing with multiple parties and documents being used as reference.

There were hundreds of questions in these audit checklists, so I wanted to move through them as fast as possible, realizing that I was pretty lucky just to be able to pull her away from training for a couple hours. So, I wasted little time during the call and was also trying to demonstrate to Jess how difficult it was getting information from the main one "holding the keys". It should be noted that Jess was actually participating in the call, not just listening in. We were both getting a little frustrated with the seemingly lack of knowledge from Mary so we would move onto the next question if the answers were not forthcoming.

So here's the point of my little story. A couple weeks later I was talking with my boss in her office about personnel matters in general when she brought up something totally unexpected. As it turns out, that conference call was not between the three people I thought it was. Mary had used an office that the Deputy Assistant Secretary (the DAS) had secured while he was at the training site and MM borrowed his office for the call. She didn't tell me that the DAS was sitting there listening in at times. I was told that the DAS thought I was being too rough on Mary, and this of course fed into the notion of creating a hostile work environment. Talk about the fallacy of the small sample! For a couple years I had worked side by side, day by day with Mary trying so hard to delicately extract information from her and build a good working relationship. And when I decide to push a little at a critical time, when she should have been back in the office getting ready for the audit, this is when upper management gets a first hand look into my supervisory skills…by spying? It's more than common courtesy to let someone know when others are on the line. I make it a point to do that and when someone should walk into my office during a conference call I let everyone know right away. It's clear to me now why Mary may have been so cautious with her responses and I don't blame her as much as the DAS for whom I lost total respect for that day.

It didn't appear to be such a big deal at the time but a few months later it was leaking out that Mary was getting moved laterally into another section of financial management, and with her went the institutional knowledge. The silver lining was that even though "the keys" (to the vault of institutional knowledge) were gone for good, we now had someone to blame for all the skeletons in the closet we found after her leaving.

I often thought back to the days when I came on board as a Staff Accountant with a really nice boss, a friendly group of coworkers and not a lot of pressure from above. Should I just have gone along with the flow, drawing a decent salary, and limiting my stress level like everyone else at quarterly closings when auditors were buzzing around? After all, it was told to me by more that one person that the non-supervisory GS-14 job was the best one to have in the federal government.   Nah…it would have been way too boring, plus I had to look out for myself and didn't feel like training a new Director and not get paid for it.

Chapter 10 - The CFO Act of 1990

Since the Chief Financial Officers (CFO) Act of 1990 the federal financial accounting requirements and objectives had greatly expanded. The stated purpose had been for more accountability and control. And it's my contention that the efforts have been a dismal failure. While agreeing in principle to the stated objectives, the way the bureaucrats have gone about the whole thing has been a pure waste of time and money.

Periodically the Act has been evaluated for effectiveness and according to the studies, it has been deemed successful but still has challenges. The people doing those studies have been the same people who have been recommending those changes and implementing them over the past 30 years. They are the financial management swamp and the swamp needs to be drained.

PROOF:

1. Improper Payments of the Federal Government have averaged $140 billion over the last three years. Therefore, controls on the spending of taxpayers hard earned money are ineffective (see Chapter 11).
2. Virtually nobody reads the numerous massive government financial reports, let alone understands them. This is with the exception of those that

prepare them and audit them. Therefore, they are essentially useless (see Chapter 12).

3. The studies evaluating the effectiveness of changes since 1990 did not consider the incremental cost of implementing those changes as described below.

Most of the significant changes made to federal financial management and reporting were based on the notion that accounting and reporting in private industry (think Fortune 500 companies) was superior and should serve as a guide for the federal government to get up to speed. The problem with that approach has been that the Generally Accepted Accounting Principles (GAAP) that the federal government was mimicking were for profit making enterprises. Someone forgot that 99+% of the government is NOT FOR PROFIT! Plus, the federal government is a huge conglomeration of highly volatile enterprises whose risk exposure (potential liabilities) can change significantly at any time. Think about it...one misstep by North Korea or Russia could suddenly result in dramatically different liability exposure for many federal entities including Department of Defense, Veterans Affairs, etc.

More precisely, the concept of a Balance Sheet compiled in accordance with GAAP (and now federal GAAP) sets forth assets, liabilities and net worth, or the difference between assets and liabilities. In order to have any real value, the assets and liabilities require support and a basis in reality; if nothing else, then at least logical estimating assumptions. If the United States suddenly declares war, what is it's liability for that? What is the liability for global warming/climate change or any other major cataclysmic disaster? The answer is: nobody really knows.

The concept of an Income Statement in the private sector (called the Statement of Net Cost in government) is to show the reader/investor how much money the enterprise has made or lost during a given period. This information is very valuable to investors for obvious reasons. The Statement of Net Cost is ridiculous in government since the government is always going to lose money, which may or not be made up by future inflows of taxpayer money.

The above two financial statements (Balance Sheet and Statement of Net Cost) form the bulk of what is referred to as "proprietary accounting" as opposed to budgetary accounting. The proprietary accounting consists of income and loss accounts, assets, liabilities, and the difference between assets and liabilities called Net Position or Equity. Budgetary accounting consists of accounts for appropriations received (funds approved by Congress and the President) and all the accounts needed to track the appropriations through the various cycles of commitments, obligations, transfers, expenditures and other miscellaneous activity such as rescissions of authority. The budgetary accounting if performed as intended is all that is really needed for good government accountability. And since budgetary accounting is highly specialized where very few understand the meaning, any budgetary reports to the public or management should be embellished with a plain English interpretation of their meaning.

Proprietary accounting is not needed for the federal government to operate effectively. Moreover, it is a cash drain of hundreds of millions of dollars every year. If the federal government got rid of proprietary accounting, that would eliminate the need for other reports and statements that are required to reconcile between budgetary accounting and proprietary accounting. Once those required statements, reports and reconciliations are eliminated, you can cut the federal financial management workforce by at least 30% and cut the Inspector General, OMB, GAO, and Treasury workforce by a similar amount. Then, you can cut the external audit fees by at least 50%. And you could probably eliminate the Financial Accounting Standards Advisory Board as well. This ivory tower group has been predominately consumed with thorny issues relating to how the government should be implementing accounting guidance that parallels private industry, such as accounting and reporting for leases. These are proprietary accounting issues which are really irrelevant as long as controls within budgetary accounting and reporting are strengthened and government spending is tracked and reported in detail as further explained later in this chapter.

In reality, the cuts could be even deeper; but what I'm suggesting, to actually improve federal financial management, would be to take some of the personnel and related resources that would have been cut and redirect them to strengthen the controls on government spending to save billions more from improper payments being made (see Chapter 11). What the government really needs is ACCOUNTABILITY not ACCOUNTING!

To be more clear, some of the existing record keeping and reporting is needed, just not all of it. To keep it simple, think of it how you would keep your own personal budget and checkbook. A budget that breaks down the functional areas of government into categories such as payroll is an absolute necessity. And to make it more valuable what is needed is an "actual to budget" comparison done periodically. You want to know what was budgeted and what was actually spent so you can plan for the future.

You also need to keep a personal checkbook that is reconciled down to the penny. And when you plan on a major expenditure, you may need to have your "significant other" approve the expenditure before it's made, right? And each expenditure needs to be associated with a budget item by some sort of intelligence built into the coding.

So take those simple concepts and expand them to fit a much larger entity but don't compromise on the controls. In fact, if the entity is really big, like a government agency, you want to keep a bunch of separate budgets and checkbooks but they all must function similarly so automated processes may be used to consolidate and report without complexity.

Right now, most of the financial systems in use throughout the government are sorely in need of upgrading. In addition, the accounting guidance that exists within Treasury and OMB is largely unintelligible by the average accountant. If you think I'm exaggerating, google "distributed offsetting receipts" in the Treasury Financial Manual. See if you can follow what on earth is going on there. The accounting of the federal government is very exacting, but confusing at the same time. Combine that condition with the fact that most of the literally millions of entries into the financial systems are made by non-accounting types, you have set yourself up for failure, plain and simple.

I want to stress the importance and practical implications of what I am proposing. There is absolutely no good reason why what I'm suggesting is not achievable within a reasonable timeframe. Plus, for all the accounting theorists that may say it's not practicable I would debate them anytime and anywhere. Their main objection will be a loss of accountability when, in fact, accountability will be improved. People will actually be able to understand how exactly the federal government is spending taxpayer money. And when a strictly controlled cash basis accounting system is fully implemented, the savings will be enormous. The following deals with the objections that government accounting "scholars" will likely raise, and the simple answers to those points.

Question: How would a transaction with a sister agency or billing to a third party be accounted for…don't you need to record accounts receivable and payable?

Answer: No. All transactions are cash basis. No credit would be extended. If an agreed upon service is provided, cash is received and the entry is an increase to cash and an increase to revenue and funds available. If an obligation is incurred, budgetary entries are made but no liability is recorded like it is now. When the obligation is actually relieved a payment is made, thereby reducing cash and increasing an expense category that is associated with a budget item.

The newly proposed accounting would eliminate all timing issues and reconciliation problems. I would estimate that by doing so, hundreds of accounting type personnel could be redirected to more productive use. This is because the reconciliations currently required by intra-governmental transactions alone chew up thousands of hours each month across the federal government. This is a fact. And like I previously described in this chapter, all the related costs of auditing, Treasury involvement, and oversight all go down, way down. I personally had spent many hours per month, as had my staff in attempting to reconcile and explain intra-governmental imbalances. A rough estimate of that just for the central office would be $5,000 per month. Then multiply that by the number of sub-units within the VA doing similar roconciliations and that brings the VA total to roughly $50,000 per month. Then multiply that by the number of agencies and departments doing similar analysis and you get approximately $1,000,000 per month wasted on reconciling receivables, payables, revenue and expense related to intra-governmental transactions. And that doesn't even include all of the related oversight and auditing expenses. How ridiculous is that?

Question: If you don't have a Balance Sheet how do you know that you've accounted for all assets and liabilities?

Answer: Each asset or group of assets would be accounted for and tracked using subsidiary ledgers. Each long lived asset such as a building would have its own ledger to keep track of costs incurred and serve as a component of an overall assets inventory. It won't be necessary to have special accounting for construction work in progress and entries to close out a completed building to a building "in service". That's because depreciation would no longer be needed. Depreciation was only really needed to spread the cost of the asset over its useful life, or to deduct for income tax purposes. For the government neither one of those is needed.

Question: What about not having a statement of net cost? How can you tell how the government entity is performing financially without one?

Answer: Since the federal government as a rule does not make a profit the statement is not needed. Financial performance would be measured by comparing actual expenditures to the approved budget. Any significant deviations from the budget would need to be explained in detail.

Chapter 11 - Improper Payments

Below is an excerpt from a Government Accountability Office (GAO) report published in 2018:

Improper payments have consistently been a government-wide issue despite efforts to identify their root causes and reduce them. Examples of past improper payments include:

the Department of Health and Human Services' Medicare Fee-for-Service program paid claims for medically unnecessary services and claims that had insufficient documentation, meaning that their eligibility could not be verified.

the Department of Health and Human Services' Medicaid program paid claims to ineligible medical providers, including those who had suspended or revoked medical licenses or invalid addresses, those who were identified as deceased in federal death files, or those who were excluded from federal health care programs.

the Department of the Treasury's Earned Income Tax Credit program made payments to potentially ineligible recipients due to its inability to verify wage information on early tax filers because of computer systems issues and because some employers filed W-2s on paper or after the filing deadline.

The government's ability to understand the size of the problem is hindered by incomplete, unreliable, or understated estimates; inaccurate improper payment risk assessments; and noncompliance with criteria listed in federal law. GAO has reported improper payments as a material weakness in internal control in its reports on the U.S. government's consolidated financial statements.

Since 2003—when certain agencies were required by statute to begin reporting improper payments—cumulative improper payment estimates have totaled about $1.4 trillion. For fiscal year 2017, federal entities estimated about $141 billion in improper payments—composed of estimates for 90 programs across 21 agencies. This total was down from about $144 billion for fiscal year 2016, but up from about $137 billion for fiscal year 2015.

Medicare programs, Medicaid, and the Earned Income Tax Credit account for about 74 percent of this total. The total of the reported estimates for the three Medicare programs— Medicare Fee-for-Service (Parts A and B), Medicare Advantage (Part C), and Medicare Prescription Drug (Part D)—was $51.9 billion for fiscal year 2017, down from $59.7 billion for fiscal year 2016. This reduction was primarily attributable to a reduction in estimated improper payments for the Medicare Fee-for-Service program for fiscal year 2017, driven by a reduction in estimated improper payments for home health and inpatient rehabilitation facility claims. Federal spending for Medicare programs and Medicaid is expected to significantly increase, so it is especially critical to take appropriate measures to reduce improper payments in these programs.

Continued agency attention is needed to (1) identify susceptible programs, (2) develop reliable methodologies for estimating improper payments, (3) report as required by statute, and (4) implement effective corrective actions based on root cause analysis. Absent such continued

*efforts, the federal government cannot be assured that
taxpayer funds are adequately safeguarded.*

The key point is that taxpayer funds are not adequately
safeguarded. And since 2003 estimated improper
payments by the government were $1.4 Trillion. That's
TRILLION with a "T". So wouldn't it make sense to put better
controls in place immediately to stop the bleeding? As
mentioned earlier, if the existing financial management
reporting requirements were scaled way back by eliminating
proprietary accounting and the resources associated with
that reallocated to stopping improper payments, the
government (and taxpayers) would save billions of dollars
each and every year.

Obviously, there are many different causes of improper
payments, but with an army of former government
accountants and auditors surely a significant dent in
improper payments could be made quickly. Keep in mind
that there would be no additional cost to the government to
do so. They could just taking existing resources from
Agencies/Departments, Treasury, OMB, and GAO to dig in
and Identify the root causes of the bad payments, then take
steps to resolve. In fact if done effectively, not only would
improper payments be mitigated but there would be savings
throughout the government by the dramatic reduction in
accounting and reporting requirements. All you really need
is budgetary accounting and detailed budget comparisons,
most of which already exists.

Chapter 12 - Useless Financial Reports

I'm sure there are a few people out there who have read the financial report of a government agency[7] or department outside of the following groups:

- Report Preparers and Reviewers inside the particular agency/department
- Auditors, Office of Inspector General, and Office of Management and Budget staff assigned to their particular agency or department
- Congress…probably just a few, who sit on committees related to a specific agency or department.

But those few outside the government who may have read a report certainly don't read much of it, and probably understand very little of what they do read, especially the footnotes to financial statements.

That is all the more reason why much of the reporting can be eliminated and nothing will change…except the

---

[7]There are both agencies and departments within the federal government. The Central Intelligence Agency and the Environmental Protection Agency are examples of agencies, while the Department of Labor and the Department of Veterans Affairs are examples of departments.

government and taxpayers could save a hell of a lot of money (see Chapters 10 and 11). The public accounting profession, the Federal Accounting Standards Advisory Board (the federal government's proxy for the Financial Accounting Standards Board, FASB), Office of Inspector General, and the Government Accountability Office may have a lot to say about doing that. Why? Because that is their life, their raison d'etre, their livelihood. I call them the financial management swamp. They have invested so much in convincing themselves that proprietary accounting in the federal government makes things better, that they will never admit that it doesn't.

In my opinion there are three basic reports that need to be maintained: the Schedule of Spending [8] (much like the checkbook described in Chapter 10); Statement of Budgetary Resources; and a comparison of the Budget for the year to Actual Outlays for the year. Of course, these three principal statements would have to be very well supported by subsidiary schedules and lots of easy to understand explanations of variances.

The other reports, footnotes, and schedules can be eliminated. But that doesn't mean you don't keep track of assets. For example, you still need to maintain closely monitored inventories of cash, property, equipment, supplies etc. But those don't need to be reported as they are now on a balance sheet. Why? Because the public at large doesn't care what the balances are; they just need to

---

[8] The Schedule of Spending reporting requirement was eliminated in 2017, thus making the Annual Financial Report even less useful.

be comfortable that the money being spent on assets is being tracked to the penny. And the way you do that is put all those extra accounting and financial types that are now surplus and put them to work making sure the government doesn't loose track of the hard earned money we pay in income taxes. Since 2003 the government has made improper payments of over $1,500,000,000,000.00. That's 1.5 Trillion dollars; Trillion with a capital T.

Each year the government could potentially save billions of dollars by shifting resources that they already pay for, and devote them to stopping the improper payments. Within a short period of time, the excess reporting and accounting could be eliminated. While that is taking place, the excess bodies doing the preparation and auditing could be identified. The best approach would be to take the smartest ones and put them on the job of identifying the root causes of the overpayments throughout the government. This makes sense because once you eliminate the proprietary accounting, reporting and reconciliations, what is left can be handled by the staff that may have a little trouble fitting nicely into the round holes of the peg board (see Preface, page 4).

After the root causes are identified, and remediation takes place, you will then be able to make further cuts in personnel. You can even get rid of some of the higher paid personnel because to maintain inventories and keep a close watch on payments won't require even an accounting degree. Of course, incentives would be necessary, both positive and negative. It would be kind of like holding a cashier responsible for the balancing the cash drawer at the end of the day. If you're responsible for a certain group of payments being made, you can be personally held accountable if a payment is made in error...anywhere from being fired to loss of bonus eligibility.

And I do realize that some payments will be made in error regardless of the new controls put in place. For example, a veteran or a social security recipient has passed away before the government, as a practical matter can know about it; and a check goes out to that person. For those cases resources should be allocated to following up to make sure the money is recouped as soon as possible. And it goes without saying that the fraud prevention and detection could also be strengthened with the money saved by elimination of useless accounting and reporting.

And yes, for those accounting types out there, accrual accounting is not necessary; the cash basis of accounting is perfectly suited for the government. They don't pay income taxes and for reasons described in Chapter 10 there is no need to track profit and losses. What needs to be tracked is every penny coming into the government and every penny spent by the government: when did it get spent; who got the money and what budgeted item did it pertain to? That's where the Schedule of Spending comes in. The statement already exists[9] but needs to be expanded to show more detail about who exactly got the money. Plus, a related disclosure about payroll would be much valued by taxpayers. It could show average salaries and benefits for certain classes of employees and actual salaries for the top

---

[9] The Schedule of Spending reporting requirement was eliminated in 2017, thus making the Annual Financial Report even less useful. It just needs to be reestablished.

echelon of leadership, much like the SEC 10K reporting requirement for the private sector.

It is so much more important to track money being spent than to prepare a bunch of meaningless financial reports and reconciliations that virtually nobody reads or understands.

As covered earlier (see Chapter 10) the government doesn't need to prepare Balance Sheets. Liabilities can't be reasonably measured, equity for the government is meaningless and assets can be accounted for and maintained separately. Take the example of property and equipment that is typically capitalized on a balance sheet. It is recorded net of accumulated depreciation. Depreciation is a concept rooted in cost accounting in order to spread the cost of the asset over its useful life.

First of all, accountants and auditors spend a lot of time deciding whether or not to capitalize assets. In the government it doesn't really matter for financial reporting purposes. The assets are already managed by other offices of government agencies responsible for buying the assets in the first place. They keep detailed records on age and condition, so if something needs to be replaced everyone will know about it and it will be put into the budget for approval. No depreciation is needed and so this is another reason not to have a Balance Sheet and Statement of Net Cost.

Lease accounting is another area where the government is out of control. Again, in the private sector there are reasons to decide whether to capitalize leases or not, but in the government it really doesn't matter. The amount of time that accountants, fiscal analysts and auditors spend figuring out the correct accounting and disclosure regarding leases is frightening. I personally spent a lot of time trying to get the VA accounting for and disclosing leases to the point where the auditors wouldn't slap us with a significant deficiency. The VA was so large and so much equipment was leased that for accountants and financial types to pull together in the same direction and present consistent and correct information was literally impossible. I sought out the supposed most financially competent unit of the VA to develop a prototype for how the lease information needed to be disclosed. It took them months to get back to me and when they did, they couldn't come up with all the lease documents, so the project died. On a positive note, there did exist an equipment lease data base at the VA, but the office running that "held the keys" and didn't like to share. Again, my point is that leases were operating just fine. There really was no reason to have to account for them like private industry. Those in charge of entering into a lease did a lot of work to accomplish that and they should be the ones responsible for maintaining the lease and renewing and budgeting for the lease payments when needed. There are so much savings here once the government financial management realizes leases don't need to be on a balance sheet or necessarily reported in footnote disclosures, at least not the way they are currently required to be reported.

To make matters worse, private industry accounting for leases was just changed effective January 1, 2019. The Financial Accounting Standards Board has determined that all lease obligations need to be reported on the Balance Sheet. This is what was previously referred to as "off balance sheet" financing. While needed in the private sector it is not needed by the federal government for reasons previously stated. However, I'm sure that as I am writing this, the Federal Financial Accounting Advisory Board and all of their staff, plus every Department and Agency are consumed with how this will be implemented for government accounting…another huge waste of time and money.

To emphasize my point I believe the personnel in most government agencies responsible for procuring/leasing buildings and expensive equipment whether purchased or leased are pretty smart. And I'm going out on a limb saying that in general, they are better suited to track and report assets than the financial management folks in the federal government. They may even be a little smarter. At least that's been my experience since they are typically the engineering types. However, there are exceptions to the rule…me being one of them!

Chapter 13 - the FPIAR Office

FPIAR stands for Financial Process Improvement and Audit Readiness. Several Government Agencies/ Departments created this special office to resolve long standing audit issues and attempt to reduce the number of audit findings. The VA's FPIAR office was staffed with a handful of finance employees, but mostly outside consultants/contractors. This elite group was supposed to be the "fixers". When a new external auditing firm was engaged about halfway through my Directorship tenure, the VA was successful in overcoming many of the old audit weaknesses. The FPIAR office was very excited about this and I'm pretty sure got some good bonuses for that since they went walking around crowing like roosters and taking all the credit.

Fast forward a few years later and eventually the auditors learned enough about what the VA was doing and oops.. back came the material weaknesses. I'm oversimplifying this but the fact is, the house of cards came tumbling down, and as of the time of this printing the VA has more weaknesses and deficiencies than ever before.

I worked closely with the FPIAR office so I know what happened and what could have prevented or at least mitigated the debacle that now exists. You may recall from Chapter 6 that VA had an antiquated general ledger (GL) system. For you non-accountants this is where all the entries are recorded for all VA-wide financial activity, both budgetary and proprietary. They also had a reporting software that interfaced with the GL but was not part of the GL, mainly because the GL was so messed up and over time really did not provide the capability of sending information to Treasury and OMB without being manually manipulated. So VA's audit report cited a material weakness in their financial management systems. Most of the manual manipulation was in the form of journal vouchers (JVs). And there were so many topside (outside of the GL) manual JVs it drove everyone crazy, not just the auditors.

In fact, the VA lost control of their JVs early-on and each year the JVs continued to build over time, and the entries mushroomed into the billions of dollars. This was because they were not only performed manually but due to the complexity and just laziness on the part of some people, the rationale for these entries was never clearly documented. Combine that with the revolving door resulting in lost institutional knowledge in Financial Reporting, and we had a big mess on our hands.

To add perspective to what unfolded, note that my Management and Financial Reporting Office was primarily responsible for the ongoing reporting requirements of Treasury, OMB and of course management and the auditors. There were many deadlines so we were always busy, sometimes working overtime. The FPIAR office and it's highly paid consultants were mainly trouble shooters, the elite; and they had their own agenda of sorts. They had their own reporting chain too; so even though we worked with them, it never seemed like we were pulling together in the same direction. The head of that office always seemed to be in competition with my boss at the time.

In any event, we had to develop a plan together to resolve the material weakness. This was the FPIAR Office's first big challenge. I knew from experience what had to be done, since my background in accounting was very different than what had been happening at the VA. I cut my teeth on preparing proper JVs and worked for a Manager that would go ballistic if he found a problem or didn't understand clearly what an entry was supposed to do. So in our planning meetings, I explained to the FPIAR office what needed to be done. There was no easy way out. Each entry outside the GL that was being made currently or carried over from a prior period needed to be investigated. The root cause needed to be determined and then dealt with depending on what was found. If a JV was found to be absolutely necessary, a clear explanation of why it could not be made within the GL would be needed and if not necessary, then reversed and cleared off the books. It was a process that would take many months and possibly years, depending on the resources allocated.

Well, that did not go over very well with FPIAR management. It would take too long and management wanted quicker solutions. So the consultants attached to the FPIAR office went to work and came up with a "better solution". It was called "Period 13". A fiscal year has 12 months of activity and therefore, 12 periods is normal. The Period 13 plan was essentially to take all of the unsupported, questionable entries as of the end of Period 12 and shove them back into the GL during a manufactured re-opening of the GL at year-end. That way, the GL would include mostly all (formerly topside) entries and they would be basically buried from plain sight. Don't get me wrong, they didn't want to hide this approach from the auditors and since the audit crew at the time was still getting their feet wet, they bought into it. I think they were just happy not to have to review and audit as many topside JVs. And technically, mostly all of the topside entries were now embedded in the GL, so that particular audit finding was resolved.

Before we officially adopted the Period 13 approach, the key management players involved had a vote since this was a major change affecting the books and financial reporting. At one meeting, when the FPIAR office found out I was planning on voting "no", you should have seen the look on their faces. They had spent easily a year developing this short cut approach and even got a preliminary approval from the auditors. I guess they weren't listening to me all along. All they were really doing was moving the problem from one spot to another. To this day I still can't believe I got talked into letting it happen, but I could read the handwriting on the wall. The FPIAR office had a bit more sway with top management and honestly, at that stage in my career I was not about to go down fighting. I had enough stress in my life.

At that point I became a real government employee. I was outnumbered and out ranked so I just went along.

Now, up to the present time, or at least just before I retired.

Chapter 14 - Government Contractors and Consultants

There are many many contractors that work in the federal government. I don't have numbers, but trust me, there are thousands upon thousands. During my time at the VA approximately 25% of the financial management and support personnel were hired under contract mostly because the regular government employees were either unskilled at a particular discipline or were too busy doing their regular jobs. That was a nice way of saying the government needed smart people in the private sector to solve problems and do the work of the 80% non-performers (see Chapter 6). And the contractors knew that, so they regarded the regular government employees as not so smart; and, for the most part, they were right. It wasn't fair to the 20% who were at least on par with the contractors if not smarter. Again, as I covered in the Preface to this book, those employees I'm referring to as not so smart are the square pegs trying to fit into round holes. I'm not using the term "smart" to measure intellectual capacity, but the ability to perform specific tasks that they may not have been trained for or have the ability to easily grasp. Plus they might just be lazy.

In any event, I had little respect for and even resented most of the contractors because of this attitude, and also because they were usually getting paid more than I was! I knew what it was like being a contractor/consultant because I was one, just prior to coming to the VA. Before the newly created office of Financial Process Improvement and Audit Readiness was created I was the primary point of contact for the contractors supporting financial reporting. In fact, it was up to me to explain what needed to be done. But when it came down to how it was to be done I didn't have the authority. I found out the hard way that their contract for services had limits. The government has contracting officers whose responsibility is to hire and manage the contract workers. I guess I should have felt privileged to see the contractor resumes before they were hired but nobody ever showed me the actual contracts or even discussed them with me. When I attempted to get the contractors to work along side us during a quarterly closing weekend, that overtime work was not in the contract. What the heck…? They're getting paid good money to learn what we were doing so they could help out and possibly improve the process, but only during bankers hours. This was outrageous.

We went through a lot of different contractors, mostly under the same firm of "WM". The principal of that group was a woman (let's call her Sam). She didn't report to me but the people she hired to support us did, albeit informally. Virtually all of the contractors provided to support the financial reporting effort had to be trained extensively. And by the time they would start to add value they would leave for one reason or another. But Sam stuck around for years. She managed to develop a close working relationship with the eventual head of the FPIAR office and had the "halo effect". I think it was because she appeared to have more knowledge than the FPIAR staff members (government employees) that she was relied upon heavily. When the

FPIAR office was established the contractors officially reported to the SES (Senior Executive Service) person in charge of that office. And because there was animosity between her and the SES executive I reported to, it was like we were on two different teams. I remember sitting in various meetings trying to pay attention to what was going on when the FPIAR staff and Sam would be having their own whispering conversations in the back of the room. They would typically just sit in on these meetings, not participate, but report back to the FPIAR executive. Just like spies, but right there out in the open…disgusting!

It wasn't until the new senior management came on board and the FPIAR office SES executive was pushed into retirement that finally those contractors were tasked to support my financial reporting team like they were supposed to all along. But by then I was ready to retire.

Contractors were everywhere in the federal government. When the Treasury Department overhauled their financial data collection system (GTAS) a major component was intra-governmental Reporting. They hired contractors to develop the software that was supposed to make it easier for agencies and departments throughout the federal government to analyze their intra-governmental transactions with sister agencies and departments. As they rolled-out that new system and provided templates for agencies/departments to input data, their contractors offered their services to train Treasury's "clients". As it turns out this "tool" they developed was for sale.

They were very sneaky about selling it. Treasury was not supposed to make money selling this type of service but there was nothing preventing their contractors from doing so. They contacted me to set up a meeting to discuss the VA intergovernmental reporting issues and how they could help resolve problems but never mentioned they were selling a product. It wasn't until the second meeting was being set up that this came out. The advantage of using their tool was that it was pre-loaded with other agency/department data from Treasury, so it was a quick way to identify imbalances and, thus, speed along the analysis. We were shocked to realize that the contractors, while getting paid by Treasury were using that platform to extract more money from agencies/departments who were obligated to report intra-governmental information in the exact format Treasury wanted and under the timelines established by Treasury.

The VA was fortunate to have someone smart enough to reverse engineer Treasury's "tool" and create our own spreadsheet tool to do the exact same thing. I don't know how the contractors were getting away with this unethical practice. Treasury should have paid for their contractors to develop this tool and distributed to all Agencies/ Departments to use for free. This is because Treasury was principally benefitting from the new system.

Chapter 15 - Government Auditors

Early in my private sector career I thought auditors from big accounting firms were pretty smart. It's probably because they paid attention in college and really wanted to be accountants. Plus, their firms put them through an extensive training program before letting them loose on clients. As I gained business experience, auditors became not so smart in my eyes. And just like any other profession, there were good ones, bad ones, smart ones and dumb ones. By the time I reached the federal government, I thought they were mostly dumb. I may have a bias here, simply because there is somewhat of an adversarial relationship between the auditing firm and its client, but the following stories give you a feel for my opinion on the matter.

Misha was an audit manager with Deloitte, the first firm during my tenure at the VA. One area the auditors had a problem with was the financial system to keep track of capital assets like buildings and such (the fixed asset system). The system worked fairly well, but one of the key reports that was part of the original design was not functioning as intended. It was supposed to be able to report the activity during the year for a class of property and sort the activity by additions, retirements, depreciation, and other changes. This would have been available for every VA station throughout the US and its territories.

I spent quite some time analyzing the report, trying to figure out why is was not working. There were so many errors in the report and illogical programming that I decided it made more sense to work with the Information Technology folks and design a new report. It was not just for the auditors because it gave management some good information on what was happening out there in the field. The new report extracted information directly from the fixed asset system and sorted the desired activity into buckets. Every penny of change/activity was identified so that the ending balance from the prior period reconciled to the ending balance of the current period being audited. And every VA location could access and use the report.

Management was very happy that somebody finally was able to produce a fixed asset "roll-forward". Not the audit manager. She was still going to recommend a significant deficiency for the VA since the fixed asset system did not have a roll-forward report that worked. She had no interest in testing our new reporting capability since the report was not generated by the fixed asset system itself. She wasn't kidding! It took a while to convince the audit partner to recognize the practicality of the new report and he eventually tasked the audit manager to test the integrity of the new report. Of course the testing was successful and the audit deficiency was dropped.

The next case involves a relatively new audit partner (I'll call her Dee) of the same firm. The VA had acquired a large parcel of land in the San Francisco Bay area from the Department of Defense (DoD). It basically consisted of an abandoned air field and the VA was intending to make good use of the land by constructing facilities to benefit the veteran in a very beautiful setting by the bay. In the private sector, this land would have been worth as much as several hundred million dollars.

The transaction for this transfer from DoD to the VA was recorded at one of the local operating centers and eventually flowed up to where I could see it at the headquarters level. It stuck out like a sore thumb. That was because the value of the land transfer was recorded at $300 million! Since it was so large the auditors had noticed it as well in their sample testing. The auditors reviewed and concluded the VA had erred by not capitalizing the land in a timely manner. And since the amount was so large it would constitute a material error, contributing to a significant deficiency finding in their report.

When I looked into the matter, I discovered that as part of the supporting documentation there was an appraisal performed to assign a value to the land. This was land no longer useful to the Department of Defense so they must have owned it for quite some time. And it was transferred to the VA without monetary consideration. It's a basic rule of accounting that asset transfers between entities of the same parent (this case being the US Government) are transferred in at cost. The cost being the same as what had been recorded on the books of DoD at the time of the transfer. So if the transaction had been properly recorded and capitalized, the value would have been something more like $1 million. So the real understatement of land capitalized would have been that $1 million, not $300 million. This $1 million was well beneath the materiality scope for a significant deficiency. Before the quarterly closing there was a meeting with the auditors where this item was discussed. Dee, the new audit partner was there and it took a while before they came around to the fact that it was immaterial. Then she asked, what about depreciation? I responded that there is no depreciation on land; and Dee said "whatever." Even after the meeting ended, they were looking at each other like...is that right? It was a real good opportunity to make fun of the auditors but I refrained.

This issue was still not easily wrapped up because DoD record-keeping for old fixed assets was either non-existent or useless. It was so bad that their auditors were not even in a position to issue an audit opinion because of it. At first I was thinking that if we could not get the carrying cost from DoD then what would we do? Then, I remembered that a couple years prior, I attended a working group session with other federal agencies/departments on fixed asset accounting. DoD had described a process they were undertaking to assign values to fixed assets based on estimates, and this was discussed with and agreed to by their auditors. It took a couple weeks to find the right person at DoD but eventually, yes, they had compiled the estimated cost for that land acquired over 50 years ago.

Once we had that information in hand, the external auditors still wanted to give us trouble because DoD did not have "actual" cost. And to save face they were still clinging to the notion that it was more valuable, thus a big error. They even had the nerve to request that we look back at similar real estate transactions over 50 years ago to see if the $1 million was reasonable by preparing comparative analysis of land sales. To make it worse, I got a call from the Inspector General's office (OIG) asking for the same thing. Since the

OIG was the office that hired the auditors, they generally supported everything the auditors wanted, right or wrong. I wasn't sure what value was added by doing that requested research, but I needed to make everyone happy. So I got in touch with our Chief Actuary and he was able to put together a statistical analysis of real property going backward in time that eventually satisfied everyone.

The whole point here is that the auditors were not really that sharp and they didn't really have a grasp on how much they cost the government in time and money chasing down information that was unnecessary or could be gathered by alternative means.

During the two years before I retired from the government the audit crew got even worse. The same Partner that didn't understand the land transfer was being groomed to take over for the Partner in charge who was retiring soon. Dee dressed like a professional but very stylish with lots of make-up. It was very funny hearing comments from the other women around the office when Dee showed up (normally a little late) for a meeting.

It's normal for audit staff turnover but along with Dee the entire audit team changed and they were taking new approaches to many aspects of the audit. I think it was because they felt duped into clearing our weaknesses and deficiencies in the past and then realized the books were not as clean as they thought. Plus, Dee was trying to make a name for herself in the government accounting area by authoring research papers and participating in committees and conferences. She brought copies of her research paper on adoption of the newly mandated Schedule of

Spending to our office. I don't think she realized the VA had already developed the report and was essentially in production. When she did find that out, I think she made it her mission to find issues with it, but to no avail.

Chapter 16 - VA's Senior Financial Management

Around the same time as the transition with the auditing firm Partner, our Senior Management was undergoing changes as well. Our new Deputy Assistant Secretary (DAS) came on board a couple years before I retired and it wasn't long before I started planning my exit. For a few months nothing really changed, but she was definitely planning changes behind the scenes. The former DAS had moved up as Acting CFO and I wasn't quite sure whether he was behind what was about to take place or if it was mostly her doing. In any event, the whole apple cart was about to be upended.

Most of us knew the weaknesses and even the auditors were beginning to find some real issues, not just the ones they sort of made up. Up to this point VA financial management had stood up to the auditors and the audit report was actually pretty good, better than most every other large Agency or Department. But our new financial management executive was looking at the long term. She didn't want to take ownership of potential problems lurking beneath the surface and didn't really want to take the time learning how and why things were done the way they were. So the path of least resistance was to give up the ship and let the auditors have their way. Every finding of the auditors was now significant and needed to be fixed.

The way the auditors presented some of the findings was actually pretty hilarious. It was a given that the VA had too many topside adjustments being made by JVs. It was primarily due to the antiquated general ledger system that was too inflexible to capture the required (by Treasury) data, plus my team was constantly uncovering errors that had to be fixed after the general ledger had closed but before reports were issued.

When the auditors wrote us up on that finding they had to make a big splash. Let's take an example where someone at the Veteran's Benefits Administration had made a $1,000,000 error in recording a liability for veterans benefits. Again, $1 million sounds large but in an organization like the VA, it was relatively immaterial. It was caught in the consolidation process and we recorded an adjustment by increasing liabilities by $1,000,000 and commensurately increasing expense by $1,000,000. That was one entry; a debit to expense and a credit to the liability. For those of you who just got lost, don't worry about it. The fact is, there was a $1 million error that was corrected by a topside (on top of the core general ledger) entry to the books. Instead of calling it just that, the auditors described it as a $2 million adjustment, by taking the absolute value of both the debit and the credit and adding them together. They ignored that fact that double entry bookkeeping is a basic principle of accounting and it's understood that every entry or adjustment has two sides, a debit and a credit.

Now, it would not have been so bad if the entries and adjustments being made were a few million here and there, but typically the VA had adjustments totaling hundreds of millions. So when you double that, it reaches over $1 billion which is so much more impressive!

All of a sudden virtually everything VA Finance was doing was in need of fixing. For the next year and a half, until I retired, we spent most of our time documenting what we did by each hour of the workday, writing corrective action plans for all findings of the auditors, and briefing those plan updates to senior management every week. I would not be surprised if that was still going on because the last audit report for FY 2018 was actually worse than when I left.

Now, you might be thinking …that sounds like a good thing to do…fix the problems. And it WAS the right thing to do, but not all at once. All issues had the same priority and needed to be worked on concurrently. Everyone working on the plans and trying to still maintain the books and records were so overloaded that no progress was really being made. We actually spent more time in meetings, updating the status of the corrective action plans, and preparing briefing reports than actually doing the work that was needed to fix things.

Our new DAS hired her former lieutenants from other agencies to crack the whip. At one time I felt like I was reporting to four different bosses. She also sent a contingent of my staff out to another agency to see how things were done…the right way. When they returned, it was what we thought; they was actually in no better shape than the VA but much smaller so things seemed less out of control. My 10 years at the VA were about to wrap up and I was counting down the days.

Chapter 17 - Catfish on Fridays

You may not realize it by now but I enjoyed many aspects of working at the VA for 10 years. Besides the steady paycheck and generous benefits, there were lots of little things I looked forward to. When I first started with the VA, I noticed my boss Jim Bob would always go out to eat, mostly walking across Vermont Avenue to an Asian buffet style place where food was sold by weight. It didn't take me long to figure out why. The VA (government subsidized) cafeteria was generally horrible, except for a few noteworthy exceptions. One great deal was the crispy bacon in the morning that was sold by weight. If you brought in bread from home you could make a nice bacon sandwich for about 75 cents. But the best deal by far was fried catfish only served on Fridays.

The catfish was so good it would bring in other government employees from all around DC even in the cold weather. It was deep fried in a light coating of batter with just the right amount of seasoning. It was very tasty just by itself but I would always dip it in a little catsup with hot sauce. I can still taste it now, just thinking about it...yum!

You had to plan out your strategy for when to eat because if you just went down to the cafeteria at noon, the line would sometimes be out to the hallway. It just wasn't fair; and to make it worse, the alien (non-VA) government workers would not just come to eat at the VA; they would pile their styrofoam containers high with as much catfish as possible and bring it back to their office for who knows how many others. For those just wanting one serving and actually working at the VA, they should have made an express line just like the supermarkets have!

The catfish sales alone may have been enough to keep the cafeteria from failing because on most other days the hot food steam table kind of just sat there mostly untouched[10] for the whole lunch period. And the couple times I tried a cold sandwich such as chicken salad, it was loaded with little pieces of gristle like they just chopped up the entire chicken with a cleaver.

The reason I'm even talking about the cafeteria is because it's another prime example of a waste of taxpayer money. The subsidy must have been enormous. Now granted, it makes a lot of sense to provide several thousand workers with convenient food service, but if you're going to do it, do it right. Make it a place where most of the employees want to go on a regular basis. They could have walked across the street and taken a few tips from the Asian place.

Even worse than the cafeteria was the "employee store." I used to peek in there anytime I was walking by and I don't think I ever saw a customer. I actually walked in one day and bought something just to see if it was really a store. I never did find out what the purpose of that was or who ran it, because they had another much larger "canteen" a couple of doors down where everyone did their shopping during

---

[10]To be fair, their turkey at Thanksgiving time was really good and their fried pork chops were thick, tender and juicy.

work. The canteen was another good story; I'll cover it in the next chapter.

Chapter 18 - The Canteen

The Canteen was a government subsidized 7-11. Except it was only open during regular work hours so employees could shop during work. There were hundreds of VA Canteen operations throughout the VA nationwide, and included cafeteria operations as well. It had everything from snacks to clothing, even underwear. It was a nice convenience and did a good business, partly because the cafeteria food was so bad, plus many employees without a lot of work to do would hang out there. The problem I had with the Canteen was not the operation, it was the accounting.

Without getting into a lot of unnecessary detail, the Canteen Fund was formed with a cash appropriation called a corpus and owned by the VA. As such it was required to be consolidated with the VA for financial reporting purposes. However, the financial management of the VA Canteen thought it was a private enterprise. Because it operated more like a retail store their financial management thought it should report like one.

The main problem here, as was the case for other units of the VA is that their financial management personnel didn't report to the central office financial management. Their Chief Financial Officer had more of a dotted line reporting relationship to the Central Finance Office and a solid line reporting relationship to the CFO of the Veterans Health Administration (VHA), one of the three major administrations comprising the VA.

Soon after I had started with the VA, I was notified that the Canteen wanted to change their monthly reporting cycle from a calendar month to a "retail calendar" month. I was still fairly new at the job but instinctively knew that sounded like it would cause problems. They had written up a proposal and I shared it with my Director at the time cautioning him that this would not be a good idea. He was the really nice guy I wrote about in Chapter 7 so he sort of tabled it for further discussion. I think he did that because about this same time his boss had left and our new SES executive was on board and officially about to take charge.

After a few weeks the Canteen CFO asked me the status. By this time my Director was on his way out so I forwarded the request to the new SES and gave her the contact information for the Canteen CFO. The next thing I know the Canteen Accountant sent me their new closing calendar and told me when their change over would become effective since it had been approved. So I started the process of figuring out how to deal with the timing differences this would create. The Canteen already was a mess because their accounting system financial data flowed through an interface to our general ledger system and it never arrived in balance. The interface had not been updated in years so until we had time to reconcile the differences, a "plug" was made to make their books balance so we could consolidate them into the nationwide VA books.

The reporting situation with Canteen got worse and worse and eventually had to be elevated up to the SES who was, by this time my boss since I had taken over the Directorship. When I explained that Canteen's new reporting calendar was reeking havoc and could potentially cause an audit finding she looked at me dumbfounded. How did that happen she asked. I told her the Canteen CFO said you had approved the change. "I did what?, she said".

I never did get the full story on who said what but the Canteen never did get straightened out to my knowledge. Since the Canteen CFO officially reported to the VHA CFO's Office, we couldn't force them to change back to a calendar month and reconcile their interface so we got the VHA's CFO's Office involved. Unfortunately, we couldn't force them to deal with it either because the VHA CFO reported to the VHA Chief Executive Officer, not the Central Office CFO. So therein lies the real problem - VA's management structure.

Chapter 19 - VA's Management Structure

If you go to one of the most recent Audit Reports contained in VA's Annual Financial Report you can see that the auditors have also picked this up as a problem area that needs to be addressed. The Canteen problem was only one small example of how ineffective reporting relationships can reek havoc on a large entity's financial reporting. The VA is really big. It has an annual budget of almost $200 billion and serves over 20 million veterans with roughly 350,000 employees. It's larger than many fortune 500 companies[11].

In order to prepare a good set of financial statements, you need all of the sub units reporting their information to headquarters the same way. This means using the same accounting policies, the same general ledger accounts, and doing it all at the same time, in time enough to close the books for Treasury, OMB and the auditors. That never happened. Why? Because it couldn't be enforced and people held accountable. Why? Because if your boss tells you it's not a priority then it doesn't get done.

Accounting and reporting has always been a lower priority than the business operations of an enterprise. In the VA's case the two major administrations VHA and the Veterans

---

[11] See Appendix B for a more detailed description of the Department of Veterans Affairs.

Benefits Administration (VBA) serve hundreds of thousands of veterans many different ways. That is the core mission of the VA and their respective financial staffs serve that mission first. The way it's structured now, the executives tasked with that mission rely on the same financial folks as we did, to serve our lower priority mission of serving uh...let me think about that one.

So what happens is when VBA financial management is more concerned with getting the veterans paid properly each month and the VHA financial management is more concerned with tracking the costs of providing healthcare to veterans, the reporting function gets neglected. After a couple years of pleading, training, and cajoling, we sort of gave up and turned the issue over to the external auditors. We, in central office, were not about to keep taking heat for the lack of performance on the part of the VHA and VBA. So we at least got the auditors to point out the weakness in the management structure that led to and continues to result in poor analysis and reporting. Keep in mind, though, that if the changes I recommend in Chapters 10 and 11 are implemented, most of this issue goes away too. The focus SHOULD be on paying the veteran, taking care of the veterans' health and financial accountability; not inconsequential financial accounting and reporting.

Chapter 20 - Size Does Matter

In the last chapter I described how big the VA is and how bad the accounting and reporting were for the two major administrations, VHA and VBA. Well, there are pockets within the VA where accounting and reporting is actually performed in accordance with the Treasury guidelines and withstands an audit without significant deficiencies. The best example is the National Cemetery Administration. Why? Because they are much smaller. The larger and more diverse the operation, the harder it is to account for everything consistently and correctly. Trust me, I know.

When I worked for the large conglomerate that was named The Columbia Energy Group I was responsible for the books of several smaller units, all of which had their act together in terms of passing audit and providing financial information to management timely and accurately. It was always fun to attend meetings of financial executives of all the subsidiaries of the Group. Virtually all of the agenda items dealt with issues of the larger subsidiaries. I was on a very intensive, year-long training program that afforded me the opportunity to see the operations of these larger units, transmission and distribution. I also got to visit offshore wells of our oil and gas subsidiary and their accounting was acceptable with the exception of their tax accounting which is another good story. Because of my performance on the training program and writing ability I was asked to write an article for the company's magazine. So, I knew how extensive and complex the operations were and after a while got to realize how and why the accounting issues arose.

The Transmission segment of the business was headquartered in Charleston, West Virginia. That by itself was a contributing factor. I'm not talking about the stereotypical West Virginians with missing teeth. I'm talking about the good old boy network that hired and retained marginally competent accounting and finance personnel without keeping up professionally or again, the square peg in a round hole concept.

Overarching all of that was the shear breadth of the organization and diversity of operations. Typically, there are literally thousands of transactions that occur every day in such an organization and they're not all the same. Combine that with the fact that many different people have their hands in the pie, so to speak, and you have accounting chaos. It was so bad at the VA that hardly anyone knew what the debit and credit accounting was, for a transaction they entered; they just picked the transaction type based on what they usually did, entered it, and if it didn't kick out of the system it was considered a done deal.

If you reduce the size of the organization down to it's most fundamental operations and smallest logical size everything can be controlled, assuming you have competent leadership or oversight. As the size increases so does the complexity and risk of loss of control. It's sort of like the "Peter Principle" where people in a hierarchy rise to their own level of incompetence within an organization.

This, however, can be combated. Divide and conquer. The key is to find the optimal size of an organizational reporting unit. While I was first attempting to analyze the VA's financial statements and changes therein, I couldn't just assign one financial statement such as the Balance Sheet to each of my accountants. There was way too much going on there for anyone to easily grasp. I eventually had to assign each Accountant one functional area of operations, such as an Administration. Even so, the VBA administration had several major operating components: Disability Payments to Veterans, Housing Loans to Veterans and Insurance provided to Veterans. Each of these had their own peculiarities in both operations and the accounting. So, ideally, I would assign one staff accountant to each distinct operating component, if necessary, in order to have a good understanding and be able to explain the financial statement changes for that component. Looking at it another way, that individual assigned to a unique complex area of operations needed to understand how every transaction recorded by operations affected the financial statements. That is the only way to identify problem areas and be able to explain changes to management and owners (in this case taxpayers). This concept is indeed challenging because of the limitation on the number of staff members I would need to have to covered the entire VA.

But there's an easier way. Wouldn't it make more sense to push down that concept into the subsidiary organizations themselves? The Administrations at the VA already had their respective staffs of accountants, so why was my Central Office staff needed in the first place? Because of what I explained in Chapter 19. Those Administration Accountants didn't feel that their primary responsibility was to have a good in-depth understanding of their financial accounting and thus, be able to adequately report up to the Central Office. Once VA management decides it's time to make needed changes this is just one of the concepts they'll have to keep in mind. They'll need to appoint competent financial management leadership and divide the responsibilities up in small enough sections so people know what they'ro doing. Once that happens the Central Office staff could be drastically cut and just serve in an oversight role like they should be doing.

It's not only the VA that has size issues. The Department of Defense (DoD) is the best example. They have never had their act together enough for the auditors to even express an opinion. They're functionally broken down between the major armed services of Army, Navy etc. but that is nowhere nearly small enough where the left hand knows what the right hand is doing. The DoD is so large and out of control it's the laughing stock of the federal financial management workforce. Even the public has been made aware of horror stories about missing aircraft and tanks and $500 hammer purchases. If ever the government will take my advice and get rid of the unnecessary accounting I've been talking about (see Chapter 10) they could save enough money to actually keep track of the things that really matter, like taxpayer money.

Chapter 21 - Reconciling to the Penny

Now given the state of the federal government's current accounting how does one actually go about making things better? With any new management shake-up or change it's always interesting to observe how change is implemented. You know there will be changes but when and how those changes are made is always a mystery at first. I mentioned the financial management executive changes that occurred during my tenure in Chapter 16. The new Deputy Assistant Secretary was very measured and laid back in her first few months on the job. She had some fairly varied past experience working for the Treasury and another, albeit smaller government department. I remember being at a couple meetings early in her tenure and she was more of a listener and we all thought she was easing into the job and it shouldn't be too drastic of a change.

Then came the wave of new hires: first naming one of her former associates in a key position at the financial operations center in Texas, and then naming a new right-hand Assistant at the Washington Central Office. She was also a former associate of hers. When I was first introduced to her new Assistant (I'll refer to her as Joan) I should have known what was about to come when I introduced her to one of my associates and was corrected by her when mentioning the amount of time she was at the Department of Energy. I was only off by a few months; evidently not good enough. So now that the DAS had her lieutenants in place, things began to change...dramatically.

I won't possibly be able to cover all of the new work we had to do but here are the highlights:

- Exhaustive list of everyones responsibilities and how often performed;
- Weekly time reports linked to the responsibilities;
- Develop documentation of "root causes" and corrective action plans for each and every deficiency noted by the external auditors;
- Brief management every week on the progress made on those plans;
- Develop scorecards for the financial management performance of the major reporting units within the VA.

Such activities are not uncommon for a changeover in management. The problem was that my staff was a production team tasked with providing timely financial reports to management, Treasury, OMB and the auditors. We knew the most about what was being done but did not have a small fraction of the time necessary to perform the requested tasks. So, we were so overwhelmed almost nothing got done.

On several occasions I would seek out what the priorities were within all these new assignments. The answer was - they were all priorities. I think back and wonder if this plan had been devised to push me into retirement; but it could not have been because I had already announced my retirement plan before all of this came down. So we ended up going through the motions, meeting target dates and attending meetings but with marginal work products. It reminded me of a guy I once worked with in the private sector who was a Manager (Charlie by name). He would bluff his way through weekly staff meeting updates, telling management what he thought they wanted to hear. It took quite some time for them to catch up with Charlie and by the time they did, he was ready to retire.

We did get some help. Our Financial Accounting Policy sister unit had folks that didn't have any real deadlines, just self-imposed ones. And the FPIAR team and their consultants were also tasked with supporting the effort. The "pigeons were coming home to roost" because those same consultants and FPIAR Office personnel who had masterminded the interim patches and fixes (see Chapter 13) were now realizing that they would have been much better off taking the long, more difficult approach to some of these problems and by this time, a few years later, much would have been solved. Everyone was on board with the corrective action plans (CAPS) but progress was like molasses. This was mainly because my section was in the best position to identify root causes, develop plans, and execute them, but we couldn't afford the time it took to do properly without compromising current reporting requirements. I never did figure out whether our CFO knew what was going on. Under normal circumstances I would have just asked him, but seeing that I was going to retire soon, I didn't want to make waves. Things were already bad enough and tensions were running high at the office every day, especially at meetings.

I got to see the true colors of our new management at these staff meetings. Our previously docile DAS would lash out at someone if they said the wrong thing. My immediate supervisor was humiliated at times and I was torn between acting professional and lashing out myself if provoked.

One of the classic run-ins with the new Assistant Joan was at a meeting concerning abnormal balances. An abnormal balance is like having a negative Cash balance. The problem at the VA and I trust most other of the larger Agencies/Departments is that there are literally thousands of potential accounts that could be abnormal because of the proliferation of general ledger accounts. The Treasury has established and maintains hundreds of them as a starting point. Then, each Agency/Department establishes sub-accounts based on the individual fund and the budget/fiscal year. I know this is way too much accounting jargon to follow but the end result is thousands of GL account balances that could potentially be abnormal. Then, with hundreds of thousands of transactions being processed each month combined with the hundreds of semi-trained people inputting them, abnormal balances should be expected. Don't get me wrong, that's not good; but it didn't happen overnight and could not realistically be expected to be fixed in the near term.

When I presented the status of abnormal balances and suggested to Joan that we are getting explanations for the big ones and working our way down to the smaller ones, she angrily proclaimed "one penny of abnormal balance should not exist" and looked at me and said "is that not right?" Yes, was all I said. I couldn't argue with that but one of the basic tenets of good management is to set realistic expectations and goals. I'm pretty sure, after three years since my retirement, that those financial executives are still there but I sure am glad I'm not. A couple of the smarter peers and staff members of mine found other jobs and the ones that were the square pegs trying to fit into round holes, who knows; I think they were oblivious to the whole matter anyway.

Chapter 22 - Telework

Telework was the government term for what I had previously experienced as telecommuting. What had been an informal practice of letting an employee work from home under certain circumstances really took hold in the federal government around the middle of my tenure at the VA, around 2010. It caught on like wildfire when people started to find out that Mary or Johnny had convinced their respective boss that they would be more productive working from home than not coming into the office at all (e.g. sick leave). It wasn't fair to Johnny that Mary had kids to watch at times for whatever reason, and his long commute wasn't efficient; and on and on went the "legitimate" reasons to telework until VA felt it necessary to create a policy for telework, with forms to fill out and everything. The top financial management at VA didn't really like the idea of employees not coming into the office, so they created rules to discourage it.

First of all, in order to telework, you had to be a satisfactory or better performing employee to be eligible. That covered virtually everyone, since to rate a poor performer "poor" required too much work. Then, you had to have the right equipment at home, such as a desk, since anyone could be issued a laptop to take home. It also had to be established whether this was telework on an ad hoc basis or a set number of days per week and a reason provided to be approved by three levels of management. None of these policy rules had enough teeth in them so my immediate boss at the time (Katie) created her own rules on top of the policy.

She gave us Directors very clear instructions that any employee who teleworks has to e-mail their supervisor when logging on to start the day and provide a work plan for the day ahead. Then, before logging off for the day, they needed to provide explanations of what they accomplished during the workday. That was actually more supervision than if the employee came into the office! So most of the nonproductive personnel decided not to telework and instead come into the office and get paid for whatever it was that they actually did. The productive employees all wanted as much telework as they could get and they generally got approved. This was because a Supervisor didn't want to lose a good employee so they both worked around whatever restrictions there were. Creativity played a large part in the justification aspects of teleworking.

So telework was generally considered a benefit to both the employee and the federal government. With the advancements in computer technology it was hard to say that most office workers really needed to be at the office. And it could free up office space (to be shared) at the same time. Telework was everywhere, so eventually OMB had to weigh-in with their own policy and rules to follow. One of the main justifications OMB cited was the ability for government to continue to function even if employees could not get into the office, for example during a snowstorm. That changed everything, at least in my office.

It snows a fair amount up around Washington DC and especially in the outlying areas where most of the office personnel live. So during an average winter, OMB would close the DC office several times, sometimes for more than one day. That would give everyone a nice day or two off to take care of kids who are home because of school closings or to just play in the snow…but NOT for teleworkers! The OMB rule was that when they closed the DC office those with telework agreements had to work from home. Well, it didn't take more than one or two snow days before most of my staff who had telework agreements decided to terminate them or not renew. Thank you OMB!

Chapter 23 - Real Criminals in the Federal Government

During my lifetime I have come across quite a few celebrities but have never gotten to know any. The same with real criminals, to the best of my knowledge; until working at the VA. At the time of this writing I'm not sure if Tom is out of prison yet, but if he is and he is reading this I want to say "Hi Tom." Tom and I got to know each other as part of my responsibility for capturing and disclosing the VA's financial exposure related to legal liabilities. Tom was the primary lawyer I worked with to capture this information each fiscal quarter.

I first got to know Tom when he was transitioning to that position. He had not yet assumed that responsibility but was sitting in for his predecessor at an audit meeting we regularly attended. I was briefing the financial management group on the status of legal liabilities and mentioned that we had not yet been provided some case data by the Legal Department. Tom stood up and starting ranting about why it was not his fault. I can't recall the exact details about that but it got me thinking about why he would be so defensive. It was not like something was being reported wrong, it was just late. After he officially assumed the role of his predecessor and realized he'd be working closely with me on these matters his personality seemed to change dramatically.

Now that he was working with me he was overly friendly and insisted that he will do everything possible to get things done correctly and on time…with my help, of course. Tom was an entertaining guy. The staff member who worked with me on legal liabilities and I always looked forward to Tom's visits. He always had a good story to tell, either about his Rolls Royces or a trip he was making on behalf of the charitable work he was involved with. We never knew quite what to believe but when he showed us pictures of his Rolls (two of them), we not only believed him but started to wonder how he managed to have this lifestyle on a government salary.

One day he brought with him a new associate, let's call her Holly. She was easy on the eyes and about 40 years younger than Tom. He explained that she wasn't officially on the payroll, but he was taking care of her, whatever that meant. She did help Tom with the clerical aspects of putting together the legal liability information so we were just glad she helped the process along and didn't question her status or how they knew each other. I seem to recall Tom mentioning about meeting her at a restaurant or bar. Tom was a very busy man. He constantly complained about being overloaded with work, so it wasn't unusual for him to seek help, essentially having others do the work for him. We all thought Tom to be a little strange, but never thought he was involved in a nefarious plot to misappropriate thousands of dollars from those who contributed to the charity for veterans that he ran.

One day, shortly after my retirement, the staff member who worked with me and Tom sent a news article about Tom being investigated for fraud. It was starting to make sense now. One of the CNN investigative reporters tried to interview Tom at his home and caught him on video speeding away in his Rolls Royce (the story is probably still out there on the internet). Evidently Tom ran a charity known as the National Vietnam Veterans Foundation. No wonder he seemed so busy all the time!

The investigators at CNN obtained tax records that showed the Foundation gave just $122,000 in cash donations to veterans in 2014 despite pulling in $8.5 million. The watchdog organizations that rated charities gave his Foundation the worst possible ratings. According to a Washington Post article dated October 5, 2017 (actual names redacted):

The former head of a D.C. charity meant to benefit Vietnam veterans, who embezzled about $150,000 of donations to spend on women he was involved with, was sentenced Thursday to five months in prison.

Tom (actual name deleted), 75, of Alexandria, who pleaded guilty in June to wire fraud, was the president of the National Vietnam Veterans Foundation (NVVF) until last year. U.S. District Judge (name deleted) also ordered Tom to pay a $75,000 forfeiture judgment, U.S. Attorney (name deleted) and FBI Washington Field Office chief (name deleted) said in a statement.

Tom admitted misappropriating $149,317 of donations marked for veterans' family members with young children in poverty between 2012 and 2016. He gave the money to acquaintances with whom he had relationships, and claimed *reimbursements for visits to clubs, meals and hotel stays that were not related to the charity.*

Tom had unilateral control over the NVVF's "Emergency Assistance Program," and could pay out $100 to $300 without oversight. The organization disbanded last year.

Evidently Tom had his hand in the cookie jar for years while working as an attorney for the VA and nobody knew about it until the charity watchdogs got involved. He was even given awards for his service to veterans and there are pictures of him with high ranking officials and politicians out there on the internet. I have to admit that none of us who worked with him suspected he was that corrupt. So, next time you see a co-worker driving a Rolls Royce, or two, don't feel too bad that you can't afford one, because chances are he or she couldn't either.

Chapter 24 - Deferred Maintenance

Looking back, it's hard to believe I spent so much time on this subject. Without getting too technical "deferred maintenance" is the amount of money it would cost to fix the things you let go over the years by not performing periodic maintenance on long lived assets such as buildings. It's like taking your car into a mechanic when something finally breaks and getting the laundry list of other things that need fixing and replacing, along with the estimate for doing it. Or in the case of your house, the estimates for replacing or wrapping all of the rotted wood because you didn't paint and caulk the exterior as often as was necessary. Since the VA had hospitals, outpatient, extended care facilities and office buildings all over the United States there was a lot of deferred maintenance and estimates ranged into the billions of dollars.

How I got involved was the financial reporting for deferred maintenance. The accounting rules at the time were not very clear and the VA had a policy but it also was not very clear. And when you have about a hundred "stations" throughout the VA reporting their respective amounts of deferred maintenance you can imagine the inconsistencies. Luckily, deferred maintenance was not required to be reported on the balance sheet as a liability, but rather only disclosed to the reader of financial statements in a back section of the annual financial report. That way, it was still an audit issue but not one that could impact the integrity of the financial statements themselves. It was not a true liability since there was not a legal obligation to incur the cost.

The main problem with the reporting was that most of the repairs needed by the VA did not technically qualify as reportable. That was because the repairs needed were often so extensive that when performed they would end up being capitalized on the books. And the existing standard was that "capital costs" are not reported as Deferred Maintenance. To properly comply with that guidance only the repairs that would be expensed would be reported. So, roughly several billion dollars of needed repairs was not disclosed to the reader of the financial statements. Does that make sense?

There was a capital asset management system which kept track of all the needed repairs. The engineers maintained that system and prioritized repairs into categories based on urgency. It was also very detailed, giving the nature of the repair, the estimated cost and the location. A big benefit was that it was also able to be consolidated by category. Therefore, the work was already done. Unfortunately there was a major disconnect between the engineers and the accountants regarding this information.

I was never happy with the way VA was reporting under the existing rules and when the government's Financial Accounting Standards Advisory Board (FASAB) took up the project I was excited to see what they would come up with. In fact, I reached out to them with my ideas on improving the disclosure and the guy spearheading the effort wanted to meet me for lunch. Surely this distinguished Board appointee would quickly grasp the issue and the accounting guidance would be changed in short order. But I forgot that this was the federal government. From the time we met for lunch until the final release of the revised guidance was issued, it was about three years…and they still got it wrong!

First of all, a committee had to be established to study the problem. The federal government is really big and, therefore, the committee was really big too. I remember attending the first meeting of that working group and between 20 and 30 individuals from mostly all of the various departments and agencies who were affected by this issue were in attendance. The tables were configured in a large square and around the tables we went, getting everyones input. After a couple of these meetings I realized that it truly was a process of managing by consensus and there was no end in sight. I soon realized that everyone on the committee had been indoctrinated in this process. Nobody ever stood up and questioned the process. It was as if this was business as usual. After the first couple of meetings it was concluded that a definition of Deferred Maintenance needed to be established so everyone throughout government could report consistently…brilliant!

This was another example of having to remind myself where I was. There was absolutely no sense of urgency. Actually, there was no sense of urgency anywhere in the federal government from my experience, except when it came to filling out time sheets so we all could get paid on time. But that reminds me, there was another sense of urgency I overlooked. That was when there was a reporting deadline and it was getting late in the day. The sense of urgency was not wanting to "miss my bus" or "miss my train".

The Deferred Maintenance project continued through the time I accepted the Director's position at the VA. Since I was becoming thoroughly disgusted with the lack of progress, I withdrew from the working group and offered up my replacement...an associate from our financial policy unit. Barry was a really smart guy and was actually a dentist working for the Department of Defense before switching over to financial management. I never was sure why he got out of dentistry but it may have had something to do with his patients not being able to keep up with his chatting. He was the type who if asked what time it was, he would tell you how to build a watch. Barry was the perfect replacement to participate in federal government working group. He was also our secret weapon to sick on the auditors. He could talk so long that eventually, everyone would come around to his conclusions just to end the discussion.

But alas, Barry too was engulfed into the bureaucratic process and could not by himself drive the consensus of the Deferred Maintenance project. After a while I think he got so brainwashed that he too lost sight of what I had been trying to accomplish. If we could just get the Board to include the costs for major repairs, in addition to those typically being expensed as incurred, it would have been so easy for the VA to collect and report them consistently, accurately and timely.

After a couple years the new accounting guidance was pre-released but without recognizing the costs of critical major repairs. When the VA had the opportunity to officially comment on the proposed revision I made one last ditch effort to get through to the Board but since I was likely the only one making this comment, it carried little weight. I was told that if VA had these anticipated major repairs to make it could create a separate disclosure for that. After hearing that, it was time to let it go.

Chapter 25 - Federal Employee Compensation

I worked ten years for the federal government, just enough to be vested in their program of highly subsidized healthcare. I am also getting a modest pension. Both of these are for as long as I live...not too shabby. Virtually all federal employees will end up retiring some day with a great pension and healthcare as well. Although in recent years there has been a lot of talk and proposed legislation as well, to reduce the federal compensation benefits. There have been ongoing debates about whether federal employees are being compensated more than their private sector counterparts. All those arguments are a bunch of hooey. There is no study that could possibly do a thorough job of analyzing that. The real issue is the fact that roughly 80% of federal employees are overpaid for their performance (also see Chapter 6). And it's also likely that the 20% who make up for the non-performers are being underpaid.

I like to think of myself as being in the 20%. That's supported by my consistently superior performance ratings, the feedback received from my peers and managers and also because I worked harder and smarter (most of the time). And I was being underpaid. I know that because I was doing a very similar job in the private sector about 10 years prior to the government job. In comparison, the VA was a lot bigger in terms of their annual budget. Their $150 billion budget at the time was over 10 times the annual revenue/expense of the Fortune 500 company I worked for. Granted, the VA did not have income taxes to account for (which was pretty nasty for an integrated energy/utility company) but the federal government budgetary accounting was equally as nightmarish. So, on balance I should have been getting paid more by the VA but I was not complaining because of the job security, the benefits, and the low pressure atmosphere. Some of my peers, when asked why they were satisfied with their government compensation (as opposed to what they could make in the private sector), would respond with the typical "it's public service or service to the veteran", which didn't make a lot of sense since there was very little linkage especially when it came to financial reporting (see chapter 12).

Chapter 26 - The Perks and Perils of Public Transportation

Another great benefit of working for the federal government was the subsidized public transportation going to and from work. Most of us got a free ride due to this generous policy. Each workday I would drive about four miles to the park-n-ride and take the bus all the way into Washington DC where it dropped me off and picked me up within two blocks of the office. The buses were really nice with high back seating and even a small bathroom (for emergency use only). And the 50 minute commute was just long enough to catch a nap or do a little reading, all paid for by the government. The buses usually ran on time and would zoom past the parking lot of cars traveling bumper to bumper on the highway. The High Occupancy Vehicle (HOV) lanes were great! Why someone would drive alone into DC during rush hour on a regular basis I could never figure out. There was a needed strategy, however, when riding the bus.

It took me several months to figure out the optimum strategy for riding the bus to and from work. In the beginning I thought that getting to the bus stop early would allow me the pick of any seat on the bus. The problem with that turned out to be you were subject to anyone plopping down beside you. The most pleasant ride was with nobody sitting beside you, so you had to figure out the least popular bus that would still get you to work on time. Then, you would attempt to avoid an overly large person plopping down next to you or someone that didn't smell so nice or someone that would want to talk too much. The buses ran out of the park-n-ride about every 20 minutes so I had a few to choose from. Then, the strategy was to make sure that I would not enter the bus until about 60% of the seats were taken. Sometimes I would just sit in my car until a sufficient waiting line had built up. And finally, when choosing a seat, I would pick one next to the skinniest person I saw and not too tall either, since their long legs would always end up bumping mine. After finding the right spot I would sit down and take a good whiff. If the person had the slightest smell, I would quickly get up and change seats. After a while I would generally get to know the people riding the bus and would pick a familiar face to sit next to.

Chapter 27 - An Army of Accountability Agents

Improper payments being made day after day by the federal government is so disgusting it makes my stomach turn when I think about the waste, fraud and abuse of taxpayers money. As covered in Chapter 11 there are well over $100 billion in improper payments made by the government every year. I personally get upset when the grocery store overcharges me by 50 cents! And when I make a monthly bill payment I make doubly sure I am being charged correctly, and am always thinking about how to get a better deal. The federal government needs more cheapskates like me!

Improper payments have to be stopped and there are no good excuses why it cannot be largely eliminated. A significant portion of the federal financial management personnel within the government would be available to support the effort once proprietary accounting is eliminated. Contractors, external auditors and Office of Inspector General staff could be used as well. There needs to be an "Army of Accountability Agents" (AAA) created to investigate and resolve each and every problem associated with improper payments. And if executed properly, the government will not only save billions of dollars being improperly paid, they will create additional savings by being able to reduce staffing in the long run. This is because the elimination of proprietary accounting will free-up at least

25% of the current financial management workforce across all of government. And of those staff that are repurposed to join the AAA some could be eventually be eliminated through attrition once the improper payments are under control.

An added benefit would arise when proprietary accounting is eliminated and the AAA is formed. Remember the 80-20 rule I explained in Chapter 6? Each financial management staff member will be given the opportunity to find a position where their experience and talents would be best utilized. The new AAA will have positions that require different skills: information technology skills to produce the financial controls necessary when a payment is processed; investigative skills to test actual payments already made as to their appropriateness; and managerial skills to supervise operations and verify and approve payments before they are made. Some of those square pegs that could not fit into the round holes of financial reporting may be better suited to follow up on potential improper payments. They can be given a checklist of the criteria for a valid payment and assigned a group of payments to investigate. Depending on the type of payment, it could be as simple as making phone calls or as involved as making site visits to the payee. Sure there would be costs associated with that but those costs would be dwarfed by the potential savings in the billions of dollars.

Recoveries of improper payments would also be the responsibility of the AAA. A system of incentives could be developed to reward successful recoveries but care should be taken so as not to unjustly enrich them if they are regular employees getting a regular paycheck.

And for the remainder of the financial management staff not suited for the new landscape they should be moved out of the federal government or at least out of financial management. I know that sounds harsh but in reality it may be the best outcome for those individuals. They may actually find a more satisfying career or take advantage of an early retirement, sweetened with a generous severance package.

Chapter 28 - Summary of Major Points

One of the main points of this book was that the federal government has a lot of fat to trim. During my tenure with the VA, a lot of folks retired and were not replaced due to hiring freezes; that was a good start. However, the financial management structure had become very "top heavy". During the last year of my employment there were as many managers and executives as staff members that actually did the work. I remember going to meetings with a room full of people doing the briefing and people getting briefed that, in total, outnumbered the staff back in their cubicles who were expected to do the work. For those of you not familiar with Washington DC, if you ever tour Constitution Avenue or thereabouts, if it's not a museum or hotel, it's a huge office building filled with thousands of government workers getting nice paychecks, health benefits and nice future retirement all paid for by you, the taxpayer. And roughly 80% of them are not pulling their weight.

The second major point is that the federal financial management swamp needs to be drained or at least rearranged. Most of the time spent by auditors, accountants, analysts, contractors and middle line managers is focused on thorny issues related to proprietary accounting, including reconciling to budgetary accounting. Proprietary accounting does not have value and, therefore, is not necessary for the federal government. As explained in Chapter 10, it just doesn't make sense. What's really needed is accountability, not (proprietary) accounting. Hardly anyone reads the financial reports issued by agencies and departments, let alone understands them.

The third and last major point is that financial accountability can actually be dramatically improved at no cost to the taxpayer. In fact, if proprietary accounting is eliminated, there will be a net savings to the taxpayer if the excess resources are repurposed to: 1) investigate the root causes of improper payments being made throughout the federal government; and 2) develop and maintain strict controls for every penny the government spends. I am confident that these proposals may be realistically accomplished in a relatively short period of time with a concerted effort. And if done, I predict that within two years, improper payments would be reduced by billions of dollars annually.

As this book is being written, the large Departments and Agencies of the federal government have many material weaknesses related to their financial systems. One of the most complicated aspects of a financial accounting system is the relationship between proprietary accounting and budgetary accounting. And reconciling between them is a nightmare; just ask any government financial reporting manager. So, getting rid of the complexity will eliminate many of the reports and reconciliations that contribute to the material weaknesses and significant deficiencies. Not only will many of the weaknesses and deficiencies go away, there is a good chance the audit report itself would become obsolete and replaced by a much more condensed opinion on whether or not the budgeting and spending information is fairly stated and developed in accordance with a dramatically reduced set of federal accounting and reporting standards and guidelines.

Epilogue

I hope to lay the groundwork for some rather radical changes that need to be made for our federal government to function more effectively. If everyone that reads this book contacts their respective congressional representatives there is a good chance my ideas will get enough attention to put the burden on the financial management swamp to justify what they are doing. I can't wait to hear their excuses.

I expect to receive a lot of negative feedback from those inside the government and those benefitting from having such a large government. People become very defensive when they fear losing something during the process of making changes or just hearing about someone wanting to change the status quo. Sometimes they lash out and act irrational like what we've seen from some of those who oppose our current President. I'll direct those comments to the circular file. Otherwise, please feel free to write me and I'll try to respond to everyone. You can reach me at smacqueen32@outlook.com.

Appendix A - The Department of Veterans Affairs Organization

(an extract from the VA's FY 2018 - 2024 Strategic Plan)

VA operates the largest integrated health care delivery system in America. The Department provides a broad range of primary care, specialized care, and related medical and social support services. It is the Nation's largest integrated provider of health care education and training for physician residents and other health care trainees. VA also advances medical research and development in areas that most directly address the diseases and conditions that affect Veterans and eligible beneficiaries.

VA administers compensation benefits, pension benefits, fiduciary services, education benefits, vocational rehabilitation and employment services, transition services, and home loan and life insurance programs.

VA operates the largest National cemetery system honoring Veterans and eligible beneficiaries and their families with final resting places in national shrines, and with lasting tributes that commemorate their service and sacrifice to our Nation.

VA provides contingency support for the Department of Defense (DoD), DHS/Federal Emergency Management Agency (FEMA), and other Federal departments and agencies during times of war or national emergency.

ORGANIZATION

VA is comprised of a Central Office (VACO), which is located in Washington, DC, the Board of Veterans' Appeals (BVA), and field facilities throughout the Nation, as well as the U.S. territories and the Philippines. Veteran programs are delivered by VA's three major Administrations: Veterans Health Administration (VHA), Veterans Benefits Administration (VBA), and National Cemetery Administration (NCA). VA is the second largest Federal department1 and has a workforce of approximately 351,540 full-time employees.

Services and benefits are provided through a nationwide network of 145 Medical Centers with hospital service, 25 Medical Centers without hospital service, 300 Vet Centers, 1,008 Clinics, one (1) Extended Care facility (stand- alone), eight (8) Residential Care facilities (stand-alone), 56 Regional Offices and National Capital Region Benefits Office (NCRBO), 142 additional out-based offices at which VR&E Operates, 122 Integrated Disability Evaluation System (IDES) offices at military installations (VR&E Operates at 71), 94 VetSuccess on Campus (VSOC) sites operated by VR&E at Colleges and Universities, three (3) Education Processing Offices (RPO), six (6) Fiduciary Hubs, three (3) Pension Management Centers, one (1) Insurance Center, nine (9) Regional Loan Centers, 135

National Cemeteries, and 108 Veterans Cemetery Grants Program funded State, Tribal and Territorial cemeteries.

.